Reinterpretations

Essays on poems by Milton, Pope and Johnson

J. P. HARDY

Professor of English
University of New England, Armidale

ROUTLEDGE & KEGAN PAUL LONDON

First published 1971
by Routledge & Kegan Paul Ltd
Broadway House, 68–74 Carter Lane,
London EC4V 5EL
Printed in Great Britain by
Western Printing Services Ltd, Bristol
© *J. P. Hardy 1971*
ISBN 0 7100 7103 5

al Rea   Research
nts

Reinterpretations

For Adelaide

Contents

Abbreviations

Preface

This book is a collection of five essays on poems by Milton, Pope and Johnson—*L'Allegro* and *Il Penseroso, Lycidas, The Rape of the Lock, An Epistle to Dr. Arbuthnot* and *London*—all of them poems of major interest to students of English literature. What is said here differs substantially from current interpretations of these poems, such interpretations appearing to me unsatisfactory for one or both of two main reasons. Either received opinion has tended to harden, somewhat, into dogma; or the analysis of a given poem's theme or structure has singularly failed to reveal what may be regarded as its uniquely imaginative centre.

This is not, however, to claim that the reinterpretations offered here are in any sense definitive. Works of art, especially those of exceptional vitality, will always provide opportunity for reinterpretation and debate. Such debate is, after all, germane to the whole activity of literary criticism. Nor do I wish to imply any ingratitude to the work of previous critics since this has unquestionably aided me in reaching and arguing out my own conclusions.

Reinterpretation does not necessarily imply revaluation in any absolute sense. No reader, for example, needs to be persuaded that *Lycidas* or *The Rape of the Lock* is great poetry. Yet my reading of *London* does imply that critics have been wrong persistently to dismiss it as an inferior work. And all the other essays do, I submit, invite some degree of revaluation in suggesting new ways of reading the poems with which they deal.

A number of friends have kindly read one or more of the essays in this volume: Mr Emrys Jones, and Professors J. D. Hainsworth, Louis A. Landa, and Maurice J. Quinlan—to all of whom I am very grateful for their helpful comments. An earlier version of the essay on *London* appeared in *Studies in the Eighteenth Century* (Canberra, 1968), ed. R. F. Brissenden, and I wish to express my thanks to the Australian National University Press for allowing me to reprint it here in revised form. I am also gratefully indebted to Professor J. H. Bishop for suggesting translations of passages from classical authors; and for assisting me on particular points I have pleasure in thanking Dr J. D. Fleeman, Professor C. J. Horne, Sir Frank Kitto, Professor R. D. Milns, Mr Kenneth Moon, Mr T. G. A. Nelson, and Dr Robert Shackleton.

My greatest debt of gratitude is to my wife, who gave me the benefit of her criticism as this book was being written. To her it is affectionately dedicated.

L'Allegro

and

Il Penseroso

The problem of interpreting Milton's famous companion poems
L'Allegro and *Il Penseroso* has been highlighted by the criticism
they have attracted during the past forty years. In 1932 E. M. W.
Tillyard said that their structure was 'one of simple progressions
and self-evident contrasts';[1] yet the contrasts are not so self-
evident that recent critics have been able to agree on what they
illuminate. Tillyard himself, admitting that he had long been
unable 'to guess what Milton was aiming at' when he wrote the
poems, connected them with the First Prolusion and an aca-
demic audience, and suggested that they represent a debate on the
respective merits of day and night.[2] Later Cleanth Brooks, recognizing that *L'Allegro* is not exclusively a 'daylight poem' any more
than *Il Penseroso* is a 'night poem', explored the symbolic significance of their 'light-shade' imagery and concluded:[3]

> In both poems the spectator moves through what are pre-
> dominantly cool half-lights. It is as if the half-light were being
> used in both poems as a sort of symbol of the aesthetic
> distance which the cheerful man, no less than the pensive
> man, consistently maintains.

I

Kester Svensden, relating the images of sound and music to a progressively developing structure, argued that 'the poet moves from communication through pagan mythology to the experience of Christian mysticism induced by Christian religious music', and considered that 'the merging of the two poems, so clearly demonstrated by Brooks from the light symbolism, is rendered more significant by this inner movement based on sound and harmony'.[4] Nan C. Carpenter has also insisted on the musical content of the poems, supposing their theme of 'the active versus the contemplative ideal' to be resolved 'through the music' and 'several musical ideas'.[5] For Don Cameron Allen, whose discussion of the poems is centred on the symbol of the 'tower', they depict not so much a conflict as an ascent: the poet 'by a continued mounting of the slopes of the intellect from common experience, to intellectual experience, to religious inspiration ... trusts to arrive at the supreme poetic gratification'.[6] And Rosemond Tuve considers that Mirth and Melancholy are the only true symbols in the poems in the sense that both are contrasting tendencies to be found in every man.[7]

There are, however, other statements, scattered throughout various criticisms of the poems, which seem to me to suggest a better starting-point for a discussion of their theme. Eleanor Tate notes that 'the role of the poet' is 'a central theme of the poems'.[8] George L. Geckle observes: 'The fact that much of Milton's early writing reveals a serious concern over the proper subjects for poetry is important in evaluating the significance of *L'Allegro* and *Il Penseroso*'.[9] And Donald C. Dorian, who adopts a narrowly autobiographical approach in interpreting the poems as Milton's 'consideration of the question whether he should suppress either the lighter or more serious side of his nature, as man and poet, for the fuller development of the other', concludes that 'they represent something like a weighing in poetry of two alternatives, either but not both capable of full development'.[10] Any of these statements might seem to anticipate what is said in this essay if it were not that the above critics develop them very differently both from myself and from one another. Dorian and Geckle, for example, take (as we shall see later) opposed views of the significance of *L'Allegro*, neither of which appears to me a true estimate of Milton's final achievement. And nowhere is cited what I believe to have been the traditional concept that in essence gave shape and substance to Milton's undertaking. The source of this is, I suggest, to be found in the two interrelated ideas that Aristotle had made current: first, that poetry can be divided into the serious and lighter kinds; second, that poets will be 'drawn by their natural bent towards one or the other'. Indeed, these two ideas are brought together in a single passage of the *Poetics*: 'Poetry split into two kinds according to the poet's nature'.[11] If these were the ideas that inspired Milton's companion poems, then we should expect them to preserve a broad distinction between the kinds of literature they refer to, and the types of worlds they celebrate or at least suggest. More importantly, however, since this distinction might easily be construed as the effect of their being mood-poems rather than as proof of their being something more, we should expect them to exhibit features that could best be explained by reference to the presence within each of them of a poet-observer, or poet, or potential poet, rather than a mere 'spectator'.

The poems' most obvious distinction between the two kinds of literature occurs in the following contrasted passages:

> Then to the well-trod stage anon,
> If Jonson's learned sock be on,
> Or sweetest Shakespeare fancy's child,
> Warble his native wood-notes wild;
>
> (*L'Allegro*, 131–4)

and

> Sometime let gorgeous Tragedy
> In sceptred pall come sweeping by,
> Presenting Thebes, or Pelops' line,
> Or the tale of Troy divine.

Or what (though rare) of later age,
Ennobled hath the buskined stage.

(*Il Penseroso*, 97–102)

Whereas the second passage refers to tragedy, the distinction in
the first between Jonson's learning and Shakespeare's untutored
genius is arguably made with respect to the comedies of these two
dramatists—Shakespearian comedy often having a woodland
setting. Moreover, the poems' other possible references to the two
kinds preserve the same broad distinction. In *L'Allegro* the names
Milton gives to his rustics—Corydon, Thyrsis, Phillis, Thestylis
—are all common to the pastoral tradition. The 'throngs of
knights and barons bold' appear in a festival context suggestive
either of courtly romance or of the mimetic 'tourney', itself a fore-
runner of the masque. And the subsequent reference to Hymen is
reminiscent of Spenser's nuptial poems and Jonson's wedding-
masques. In *Il Penseroso* there is a reference to Musaeus, the legendary founder of Greek priestly poetry, who is addressed by the
sibyl in *Aeneid* VI as *optime vates* (l. 669); to Chaucer's unfinished
Squire's Tale (and perhaps its continuation by John Lane, the friend
of Milton's father);[12] and to

aught else, great bards beside,
In sage and solemn tunes have sung,
Of tourneys and of trophies hung;
Of forests and enchantments drear

(116–19)

—presumably an allusion to the epics of Ariosto, Tasso and
Spenser.

The companion poems' several references to Orpheus and his
music, in reflecting two very different perceptions of the same
story, nicely underline the distinction suggested above. The passage in *L'Allegro*, lyrical in tone, emphasizes the possibility of a
happy ending in the imagined reunion of the lovers, with Orpheus
awaking from 'golden slumber' (an echo from Dekker's comedy
Patient Grissil)

4

on a bed
Of heaped Elysian flowers

(146–7)

to hear strains of 'linked sweetness' that would have 'quite set free' his beloved Eurydice. In *Il Penseroso*, Orpheus attempts to rescue Eurydice from the underworld by singing 'such notes' (presumably 'most musical' and 'most melancholy') as

warbled to the string,
Drew iron tears down Pluto's cheek,
And made hell grant what love did seek.

(106–8)

Yet far from suggesting a happy ending, these lines contain a final, tragic, irony.

Many of the 'unreproved pleasures free' (l. 40) of *L'Allegro* are such as a young poet dedicated to the countryside and its world of youth and young love would naturally celebrate. The whole pastoral tradition is an important source of the poem, which has been variously linked with the 'come-live-with-me' motif and the theme of the ideal pastoral day.[13] But the tone of parts of the poem clearly derives from a different source. *L'Allegro* evokes, though with considerable sophistication, the sights and sounds of the native pastoral and the folk fairy-lore of the English countryside. It also evokes a more courtly world reminiscent of sophisticated comedy and romance. The description of the ploughman, milkmaid, mower and shepherd is followed by an enumeration of 'new pleasures' that have caught L'Allegro's 'eye'; and here the bucolic and courtly are juxtaposed. Even without the echo ('daisies pied') from *Love's Labour's Lost*, one is conscious of a statelier landscape:

> Towers, and battlements it sees
> Bosomed high in tufted trees,
> Where perhaps some beauty lies,
> The cynosure of neighbouring eyes.
>
> (77–80)

Of course, L'Allegro's steps are at this point still set in paths of more obvious rusticity, as the subsequent lines make clear:

> Hard by, a cottage chimney smokes,
> From betwixt two aged oaks,
> Where Corydon and Thyrsis met,
> Are at their savoury dinner set
> Of herbs, and other country messes . . .

But when the countryside and its homely pleasures are at last 'lulled asleep' (l. 116), he moves easily, if only in imagination, into a more sophisticated and ceremonious, though no less lovely, world. The presence of both worlds in the poem, and the skill with which they are blended, it is tempting to attribute to the fact that each represents a possible source of inspiration for the young poet who finds himself drawn by his natural bent towards the lighter of the two literary kinds.

Milton's description of *L'Allegro*'s presiding goddess is arguably consonant with such a reading of the poem:

> come thou goddess fair and free,
> In heaven yclept Euphrosyne,
> And by men, heart-easing Mirth,
> Whom lovely Venus at a birth
> With two sister Graces more
> To ivy-crowned Bacchus bore;
> Or whether (as some sager sing)
> The frolic wind that breathes the spring,
> Zephyr with Aurora playing,
> As he met her once a-Maying,
> There on beds of violets blue,

6

And fresh-blown roses washed in dew,
Filled her with thee a daughter fair,
So buxom, blithe, and debonair.

(11–24)

This figure recalls Dame Gladnesse in Chaucer's *Romaunt of the Rose*,[14] who is represented as having the gift of song:

Wel coude she synge and lustyly,—
Noon half so well and semely . . .
For she was wont in every place
To syngen first, folk to solace.
For syngyng moost she gaf hir to;
No craft had she so leef to do.

(747–8, 755–8)

And in Jonson's *Part of the King's Entertainment in passing to his Coronation*, Euphrosyne, or 'Gladnesse', is represented as having 'at her feet a tymbrell, harpe, and other instruments, all ensignes of gladnesse' (ll. 131–2). Significant, too, is her parentage as Milton describes it. This in classical mythology had been variously recorded. Of the traditions open to him, Milton, however, followed that which most clearly linked Euphrosyne with poetry. Bacchus is 'ivy-crowned'; as one who inspired poetry, this figure was traditionally associated with the dithyramb and comedy.

Quid quereris refugam vino dapibusque poesin?

asks Milton in his *Elegia Sexta*;

Carmen amat Bacchum, carmina Bacchus amat.

(13–14)

As this *Elegy* goes on to illustrate, Bacchus is both a subject for and an inspirer of poetry, being mentioned, with Venus, as one of the deities who 'look after light-footed elegy'.[15] Venus, too, as goddess of Love, can be interpreted as fittingly associated, if only

7

through her daughter, with a kind of poetry in which the theme of love is so pervasive, and of which, on my reading of L'Allegro, Euphrosyne appears as the 'Muse'.

But Bacchus and Venus could both have less attractive, even ignoble, associations, and it may have been for this reason that Milton, by temperament Apollonian, suggested for Euphrosyne a parentage of his own invention. Zephyr and Aurora were also figures appropriately symbolic for his purpose, both having appeared as attendants of Maia in Jonson's *Entertainment at Highgate*, where the special powers of each help to adorn the spring.[16] Of more significance is the fact that Zephyrus had, from classical times, appeared in a pastoral setting, and that Milton had, in his Second Prolusion, described Aurora as 'the friend of the Muses' (*Aurora Musis amica*). Nor need one assume that the young scholar was merely making a debating-point, for the 1608 edition of Vincenzo Cartari's *Le Imagini de i dei degli antichi* had reproduced Aurora in a chariot drawn by Pegasus to indicate dawn as the best hour for poetic composition.[17]

If the pastoral element in *L'Allegro* reflects a creative sensibility that is to be associated with the lighter kind of poetry, what, then, of its companion piece *Il Penseroso*, which some critics have also linked with the pastoral tradition? Sara Ruth Watson, for example, has claimed that both poems 'are concerned with an ancient and well established pastoral theme, that their personal and melancholy elements are rooted in the tradition of pastoralism, and that their form or organization first received full expression by Virgil'.[18] But *Il Penseroso* is unlike anything to be found in the pastorals of Virgil or Tibullus or Spenser or Drayton or Browne. What marks it off from the pastoral is evident even in those passages where the resemblance is most apparent:

> 'Less Philomel will deign a song,
> In her sweetest, saddest plight,

Smoothing the rugged brow of night,
While Cynthia checks her dragon yoke,
Gently o'er the accustomed oak.

(56–60)

Again, beginning at line 131 ('And when the sun . . .') is a passage
containing the familiar trappings of Silvanus and the nymphs, and
suggestive of the pastoral commonplace of shelter and rest from
the noonday sun. Here, however, the pastoral scenery, having
more to offer than merely shelter and rest, effectively provides the
opportunity for 'some strange mysterious dream'. That this is to
be interpreted as a 'dream' of poetic inspiration will be suggested
later.

What is reminiscent of the pastoral convention in *Il Penseroso*
can largely be explained by the traditional association of poet and
shepherd—a tradition Spenser, for example, had used to record
his estimate of contemporary poets.[19] But to look for other parallels to the pastoral tradition in *Il Penseroso* seems to me to obscure
the very different source from which this poem springs. We do not
find in it the following kind of dissociated sensibility so characteristic of the conventional pastoral:[20]

Nor would I wish thee so thy self abuse
As to neglect thy calling for thy Muse,
But let these two so each of other borrow,
That they may lessen mirth, and lessen sorrow.

Nor does Milton find it necessary to parade any recognition of that
sharp division between pastoral and heroic strains which is variously expressed by Spenser and Browne.[21] Even the practical lore
that the shepherd of Spenser's *December* acquires, as 'the springe'
of life 'gives place to elder time', is very different from the philosophical wisdom and divine knowledge that Il Penseroso hopes to
attain. In Drayton, too, the elderly Borrill, convinced that love is
a deceit, devotes himself instead to 'the shepheards nice astro-
lobie'; and this shepherd has other pursuits, superficially **more**

9

in keeping with those described in *Il Penseroso*, to offer his young
and scornful companion:[22]

> Or if thou wilt in antique Romants reede,
>   of gentle Lords and ladies that of yore,
> In forraine lands atchiev'd their noble deede,
>   and been renownd from East to Westerne shore.

Yet Milton's poem presents a man unsoured by experience, who is
consciously seeking to cultivate a creative affinity with the universe
in order that he may one day be able to give inspired utterance
to a more exalted theme. Study and reading is not just something that he turns to when the delights of youth have passed. On
the contrary, the task he sees before him demands both his life-
long dedication and, finally, a setting that allows all the knowledge,
wisdom and inspiration born of his observation and experience to
reach a full and proper maturity:

> And may at last my weary age
> Find out the peaceful hermitage,
> The hairy gown and mossy cell
> Where I may sit and rightly spell
> Of every star that heaven doth shew,
> And every herb that sips the dew;
> Till old experience do attain
> To something like prophetic strain.
>
> (167–73)

That 'prophetic' here means 'pertaining or proper to a prophet
or inspired bard' may, I think, be safely assumed. 'Prophet' as the
equivalent of *vates* was already in use by Milton's time—though
the best illustration of this meaning postdates *Il Penseroso*, occur-
ring in *Mr Robert Herrick's Farewell unto Poetry*:

> Homer, Musaeus, Ovid, Maro, more
> Of those god-full prophets long before
> Hold their eternal fires.
>
> (41–3)

Thus, in view of this arguably explicit reference to the poetic vocation at the end of *Il Penseroso*, it seems to me obvious what Milton's companion poems are about. In them comedy and tragedy (or epic) are mentioned not, I suggest, as indications of what may appeal to the different moods of a detached 'spectator', but as inspirational examples of both literary kinds which L'Allegro and Il Penseroso as poets, or potential poets, respectively propose to themselves. The poems' differing worlds may be regarded as reflections of two separate moods in the very special sense that they are projections of what were traditionally regarded as opposite and mutually exclusive sides of the poetic temperament. Such an interpretation of the poems' theme does not, however, depend solely on the evidence already presented. It derives further support both from *Il Penseroso*'s use of the Renaissance tradition of creative Melancholy, and from certain other features of the poems to be discussed later in this essay.

Various modern scholars have discussed the significance of 'divinest Melancholy'.[23] They cite a number of Renaissance authors who, elaborating on the view attributed to Aristotle, established an alternative to the Galenic, humoral tradition by claiming that melancholy indicated intellectual and imaginative powers, and was a characteristic of philosophers, poets, and other creative artists. Of these authors the most influential was Marsilio Ficino, the Florentine humanist, who seems to have been the first to link the melancholy caused by Saturn with the Platonic 'divine frenzy' or *furor poeticus*.[24] Later Burton was to give currency to the same idea by asserting that melancholy causes 'many times a divine ravishment, and a kind of *enthusiasmus*, which stirreth [men] up to be excellent philosophers, poets, prophets, etc.'.[25] Perhaps the most accessible and best known account to students of Milton is Miss Tuve's, who aptly describes the Melancholy of *Il Penseroso* as 'a patron "Saint" of those whose desire is to understand the mysteries of things, and who practise poetry as a high form of contemplative knowledge'—or, more simply, as 'a goddess of the Imagination'.[26]

Milton's description of Melancholy is an original reworking of various aspects of the whole, complex tradition. The Neoplatonist Ficino had stated that Saturn signifies 'divine contemplation', leading the philosophical mind to higher and more hidden matters: *omnium planetarum altissimus, investigantem evehit ad altissima*.[27] Milton invented Melancholy's other parent Vesta, who imparts to the portrait of his 'goddess' appropriate connotations of chaste seclusion, constancy of mind, and pure, celestial fire.[28] In describing Melancholy's appearance, Milton, as has been pointed out, tellingly transforms certain details derived from medical and scientific literature:[29]

Her 'facies nigra' is only an illusion of our weak senses, which cannot stand the brilliance of her true aspect. . . . Her 'leaden downward cast' is only the sign of complete absorption—nothing but the reverse side of a condition of ecstatic, visionary trance.

The morbid rigidity of the melancholic is wonderfully metamorphosed in 'Forget thyself to marble . . .', an idea which, though it originates in the Niobe legend, echoes Milton's rapt appreciation of Shakespeare's work:[30]

Then thou our fancy of itself bereaving,
Dost make us marble with too much conceiving.

Moreover, unlike the Dame Mérencolye of French romance, who appeared in disordered and ragged clothing, Milton's Melancholy is clad

All in a robe of darkest grain,
Flowing with majestic train.

(33-4)

And she is surrounded not by the 'grim women Deffiance, Indignation and Désesperance', but by Peace, Quiet, 'spare Fast' ('that oft with gods doth diet'), Leisure, the 'cherub Contemplation', and the 'mute Silence'[31]—unless, that is, 'Philomel will deign a song'. This introduction of the nightingale, which here effects a felicitous transition from the allegorical mode to the naturalistic, can be interpreted as a significant indication of Milton's theme. In an important sense it confirms the emphasis that the transformation of traditional elements has given to this portrait of Melancholy. As John Leon Lievsay has pointed out, Milton, in his repeated references to the nightingale, regarded it as a symbol of his own poetic voice.[32]

If the reader does not overlook the hints contained in these fifty or so lines, he will, I suggest, be disposed to regard the rest of the poem as alluding not merely to scenes of reflective solitude that the Melancholy Man enjoys, but to moments of creative solitude that provide fitting inspiration for the poet disposed to dedicate himself to literature of a serious kind. But what of lines like the following?

> Oft on a plat of rising ground,
> I hear the far-off curfew sound,
> Over some wide-watered shore,
> Swinging slow with sullen roar;
> Or if the air will not permit,
> Some still removed place will fit,
> Where glowing embers through the room
> Teach light to counterfeit a gloom,
> Far from all resort of mirth,
> Save the cricket on the hearth,
> Or the bellman's drowsy charm,
> To bless the doors from nightly harm.
>
> (73–84)

It is, perhaps, unwarranted to hear in these lines dim anticipations of a Gray's *Elegy* or a Coleridge's *Frost at Midnight*. Yet the kind of sensibility they reflect arguably belongs to a poet, or potential poet, rather than a mere 'spectator'. John Carey, the poem's recent editor, has noted that 'sullen roar' is reminiscent of

Northumberland's words at the moment when he is about to learn
of his son Percy's death:

> his tongue
> Sounds ever after as a sullen bell,
> Rememb'red tolling a departing friend.
>
> (*2 Henry IV*, I. i. 101-3)

And even if this should be regarded as too distant an echo to indicate Il Penseroso's conscious recollection of the Shakespearian
passage, the reference to the 'bellman' may remind us that Herrick
was later to describe as follows the very act of poetic composition:

> We who have spent our time
> Both from the morning to the evening chime,
> Nay, till the bellman of the night had tolled
> Past noon of night, yet wear the hours not old
> Nor dulled with iron sleep, but have outworn
> The fresh and fairest flourish of the morn
> With flame and rapture . . .
>
> (*Farewell unto Poetry*, 15-21)

Moreover, Milton's subsequent lines express Il Penseroso's wish
to emulate in study—and hence the knowledge or power this con-
fers—those ancient philosophers whom Miss Tuve has rightly
identified as 'the major figures in that group of *prisci theologi* who
were thought to have foreshadowed Christian revelation':[33]

> Or let my lamp at midnight hour,
> Be seen in some high lonely tower,
> Where I may oft outwatch the Bear,
> With thrice great Hermes, or unsphere
> The spirit of Plato to unfold
> What worlds, or what vast regions hold
> The immortal mind that hath forsook
> Her mansion in this fleshly nook.
>
> (85-92)

This description of intellectual endeavour, and of the divine knowledge it leads to, may, as Allen has pointed out, be taken to recall that passage in the *Poimandres* which describes the 'immortal mind' ascending to the eighth sphere, where it 'sings, together with those who dwell there, hymning the Father'.[34] It would therefore seem plausible to suggest, especially since Milton regarded 'Voice and Verse' as 'sphere-borne harmonious sisters' (*At a Solemn Music*, l. 2), that Il Penseroso's wish to possess an intimate acquaintance with the 'immortal mind' in its final dwelling-place signalizes his poetic, and not just his philosophic, aspirations.

Certain features of the companion poems have presented something of a puzzle to critics content to read them simply as a contrast between two moods, or as exhibiting the contrasting dispositions towards mirth and melancholy to be found in every man. But these features—which are here considered in turn—make for no difficulty of interpretation if the poems are read as a contrast between two different kinds of poetic sensibility, or two different kinds of creative potential enjoyed respectively by L'Allegro and Il Penseroso as poets, or potential poets.

Though Dr Johnson viewed the poems as distinguishing between two 'dispositions of mind', he also thought that the poet had not kept these 'sufficiently apart': 'No mirth can, indeed, be found in his melancholy; but I am afraid that I always meet some melancholy in his mirth'.[35] J. B. Leishman, in taking up Johnson's point, has also noted a 'certain disparity between programme and performance, between what we are led to expect [from the introductory stanzas] and what we actually get'. In brief, he sees these stanzas as a banishing of extremes, and the poems that follow as exemplifying 'the pleasures appropriate to two contrasted but complementary moods'.[36] Each introductory stanza can obviously be contrasted with the rest of the poem in which it appears, with the introductory stanza of the companion poem, and with what the companion poem itself celebrates. But there is also in the introductory stanzas a point of comparison in that each alludes, directly or indirectly, to Morpheus's Cave of Sleep. And these allusions may further be contrasted with a 'sleep' or 'dream' motif that emerges in each of the companion poems briefly. This motif, I suggest, embodies that which precludes any sharp tonal contrast between these poems, and may better explain the effect that critics have described in terms of their 'merging', or of their 'complementary moods'.

In *L'Allegro* the lines

> There under ebon shades, and low-browed rocks,
> As ragged as thy locks,
> In dark Cimmerian desert ever dwell
>
> (8–10)

recall Ovid's description of the home of Morpheus 'near the land of the Cimmerians' (*prope Cimmerios*).[37] In the introductory stanza of *Il Penseroso*, Morpheus is mentioned by name in a passage which perhaps owes something to Ovid's description, but which more clearly echoes Sylvester's translation of Du Bartas's description of the Cave of Sleep. And in each poem there is an initial contrast between the Morphean motif of the introductory stanza and the lines that follow. In Ovid's description of the *ignavi domus . . . Somni*, 'no wakeful, crested cock with his loud crowing summons the dawn'; but the world of *L'Allegro* is awakened as

> the cock with lively din,
> Scatters the rear of darkness thin.
>
> (49–50)

In *Il Penseroso*, where the reference to Morpheus is explicit, Milton metamorphoses the 'mute Silence' (*muta quies*) that inhabits the Ovidian abode into a companion of Melancholy herself. Yet the full significance of the contrast between the introductory stanzas and the poems proper is ultimately to be understood in terms of what this latter metamorphosis symbolizes. In direct opposition to the crass, sluggish, Morphean sleep (in Sylvester this god is surrounded by 'blear-ey'd Sleep', Oblivion, and 'nasty Sloth'), the poems themselves describe an altogether more creative kind of 'sleep' or 'dreaming':

> Such sights as youthful poets dream
> On summer eves by haunted stream;
>
> (*L'Allegro*, 129–30)

> . . . Entice the dewy-feathered Sleep;
> And let some strange mysterious dream,
> Wave at his wings in airy stream,
> Of lively portraiture displayed,
> Softly on my eyelids laid.
>
> (*Il Penseroso*, 146–50)

While the lines from *L'Allegro* recall the tradition of poetic dream-visions, those from *Il Penseroso* seem also to refer to a 'dream' of poetic inspiration. 'Strange' may connote a 'dream' that is not only unfamiliar or rare, but excites an exceptional degree of wonder or astonishment. The meaning of 'mysterious' is more difficult to determine, and may be (according to the *OED*) either 'of obscure origin, nature or purpose', or 'wrapt in or fraught with mystery'. If Milton is describing a 'dream' of poetic inspiration, of which the origin, nature or purpose is in some sense known, 'mysterious' arguably refers to what the 'dream' reveals, namely, the kind of truth or knowledge that results from something akin to divine revelation. And that such a 'dream' could properly be experienced by a poet is suggested not only by Milton's later reference to 'something like prophetic strain' (l. 174), but also by his conception, as expressed elsewhere in his works, of poetic inspiration.[38] In addition to those passages of *Paradise Lost* which refer to the 'nightly visitation' of his Muse (IX. 22; cf. III. 29–32, VII. 28–31), one may cite examples of this imagery from works that belong to the same period as his companion poems. In *Elegia Quinta* he associates with the return of spring the return of his own poetic powers, when 'at night my dreams bring Pirene to me' (*mihi Pyrenen somnia nocte ferunt*). In *Ad Patrem* he refers to his verses as

Hypocondriacism

'the fruit of dreams dreamt in a cavern far away, fruit of the laurel groves in a sacred wood, of the shady groves on Parnassus' (ll. 15–16). And in his Seventh Prolusion, he links 'a cultured and liberal leisure' (*erudito & liberali otio*) with *divinum Hesiodi somnum*, the 'holy (or prophetic) sleep of Hesiod', to whom the Muses 'one day taught glorious song while he was shepherding his lambs under holy Helicon'.[39]

What, then, seems subtly suggested by Milton's use of a 'dream' motif in *L'Allegro* and *Il Penseroso* is that the moods banished in the introductory stanzas are both alien or even hostile to those 'dreams' or moods of poetic creativity with which the poems proper are concerned. Atrabilious melancholy, and the dreams it traditionally produced,[40] would have been at the furthest possible remove from the 'dream' or mood appropriate to the poet-observer who, because of his age ('youthful') and joyous temperament, will naturally be drawn towards the youthful and joyous world of the lighter kind of poetry. Nor is the 'dream' of poetic inspiration alluded to in *L'Allegro* at all comparable with those 'gaudy', 'fickle' dreams associated with 'vain deluding Joys', and appropriately put to flight in the introductory stanza of the companion poem. Indeed, Milton seems to be explicitly suggesting that the 'strange mysterious dream' desired by Il Penseroso can only occur after the Morphean world has been completely banished.

Another feature of the companion poems that has presented something of a problem to critics is their syntax. John Crowe Ransom, for example, has spoken of 'long sentences with difficult grammatical references, and uncertainty as to whether the invocation has passed into the action, and as to just where we are in the action'.[41] In *L'Allegro*, especially, the comparative absence of the first person, singular, of the personal pronoun is perhaps one reason why Brooks has talked in terms of 'aesthetic distance'; so little use is made of 'I' that the 'spectator' may well seem very detached indeed! Johnson, too, in giving currency to the term 'spectator', was probably aware of the same thing:[42]

> The man of *cheerfulness*, having exhausted the country, tries what 'towered cities' will afford, and mingles with scenes of splendor, gay assemblies, and nuptial festivities; but he mingles a mere spectator as, when the learned comedies of Jonson or the wild dramas of Shakespeare are exhibited, he attends the theatre.

The problem has, in fact, been notoriously highlighted by Robert Graves, who has suggested that Milton misplaced sixteen lines (53–68) which should have followed line 114.[43] Graves seeks to justify this totally unjustifiable suggestion on two grounds: first, that Milton forgot, when he represented himself as 'walking not unseen' in line 57, that he was 'still supposedly standing naked at the open window'; second, that these lines only make sense if they are rearranged so that 'oft list'ning' and 'not unseen' can be taken to refer to the 'lubber fiend'.

What Graves takes exception to in this one passage is, after all, a common feature of the poem's syntax. From lines 37–8—

> And if I give thee honour due,
> Mirth, admit me of thy crew—

to the 'come-live-with-me' formula of the final couplet, the first personal pronoun occurs only four times: 'my' (l. 46), 'mine' (l. 69), 'us' (l. 117), 'me' (l. 136). The first of these occurrences, when L'Allegro is 'bid good morrow', may be taken to represent his necessary introduction to the world that Mirth's 'crew' inhabits. The second ('mine') may be taken to individualize the appropriate surprise and delight that he, as a new member of Mirth's 'crew', feels on seeing 'new pleasures'. And the 'us' may be taken to demonstrate that he is one of a group. The apparent detachment is really no detachment at all since what is being signalized is his enjoyment of Mirth's 'delights' in company with other devotees.

Not until line 136 is one made aware of some degree of individualized consciousness, and even here, where the first person, singular, of the pronoun may be taken to anticipate an act of individual creativity, the suggestion is of an inspiration that comes from that which surrounds and encompasses the speaker. Perhaps his identity has thus far been deliberately subordinated to his surroundings in order to create the effect of senses so openly alive to the scenes before him that what is suggested is a poet's consciousness rather than the detached sensibility of a mere 'spectator' who remains aloof from that which the poem describes. Indeed, one may carry the argument a step further and suggest that this immediacy of response as one of a group can be readily associated with poetry of the lighter kind, with its direct appeal to the emotions and its characteristically communal activity of patterned harmony. In *Il Penseroso*, on the other hand, though the experiences are no less convincingly realized, the reader is always conscious of a creative intelligence that is fostered by solitude. And here one may further suggest that what is implied is an awareness of the deeper complexities of human existence that can only find fitting expression in poetry of the serious or epic kind.

Perhaps the best evidence for reading these poems in the way already suggested is provided by their explicit references to music. The following passage (placed between the examples of Shakespeare and Orpheus) represents the climax of *L'Allegro*'s 'delights':

> And ever against eating cares,
> Lap me in soft Lydian airs,
> Married to immortal verse
> Such as the meeting soul may pierce
> In notes, with many a winding bout
> Of linked sweetness long drawn out,
> With wanton heed, and giddy cunning,
> The melting voice through mazes running;

> Untwisting all the chains that tie
> The hidden soul of harmony.
>
> (135–44)

Miss Carpenter suggests that these lines 'describing the "soft *Lydian* Aires, Married to immortal verse" call strongly to mind the florid Italian aria with its virtuoso passages, trills, roulades'.[44] And Miss Tuve exclaims: 'Where are we? and whence, and when, does the music sound? This is not *the joyful man's day*. It is *Joy*.'[45] My concern with the passage, however, is to see whether the stated effect of such music can lead us to any more precise idea of its origin. The person who hears this music as something outside himself seems to be Orpheus rather than L'Allegro, whose deeper involvement with it is suggested both by the diction and imagery, and by the syntactical complexity of the first few lines (where 'married to immortal verse' can be taken with 'me' as well as with 'Lydian airs'). Given the adjacent references to Shakespeare and Orpheus, the legendary poet-singer of antiquity, as well as the traditional analogy between music and poetry (which, for example, finds expression in *Ad Patrem*), it seems likely that Milton is here referring not just to L'Allegro's delight in a certain type of vocal music, but to his aspiration towards that which is described, in a special sense, as 'the hidden soul of harmony'. This phrase, together with the previous image of the 'meeting soul', recalls the Pythagorean doctrine of a universal harmony, the Renaissance believing that music could induce such a state of rapture and refined perception as lifted the individual soul to the divine.[46] Significantly Milton had not only defended this idea in his Second Prolusion, but given it a Christian context in his *Nativity Ode*, where he refers to the effect of the celestial music on the 'fancy':

> For if such holy song
> Enwrap our fancy long,
>   Time will run back, and fetch the age of gold.
>
> (133–5)

As we learn from *Paradise Lost*, 'fancy' is the faculty that 'forms imaginations'

of all external things,
Which the five watchful senses represent.

(V. 103–4)

If, then, it is legitimate to interpret the passage in *L'Allegro* as referring to the heights which the poetic fancy may attain, it can be read as the anticipated culmination of a mental process which, from an initial perception of sensory objects, looks forward to a more spiritual communion with the divine in its creation of a world of poetry that uniquely embodies the universal harmony of the Golden Age.

The following conceit in Milton's Second Prolusion (*On the Harmony of the Spheres*) arguably finds an echo in his companion poems: 'It is in order to tune their own notes in accord with that harmony of heaven to which they listen so intently that the lark takes her flight up into the clouds at daybreak and the nightingale passes the lonely hours of night in song.' If the nightingale of *Il Penseroso* may be regarded as a symbol of the poetic voice in a certain mood, then presumably the lark of *L'Allegro* may be regarded as symbolic of the poetic voice in another mood. And in each poem it is a poet-observer or potential poet, and not just a musically-inclined 'spectator', who wishes to be affected by the celestial harmony, and anticipates having his soul (in accordance with the familiar and bizarre image) drawn out of his body through the ear by such music.

A clearer echo still of the Second Prolusion in *Il Penseroso* can be taken in conjunction with Milton's *Elegia Sexta* to suggest those strains which the Melancholy Poet aspires to sing. In the Second Prolusion Milton, referring to that passage in Hesiod where the Muses of Helicon are described as dancing around the altar of 'the mighty son of Saturn', attributes the origin of this fiction to the celestial harmony. In *Il Penseroso*, 'spare Fast', one of Melancholy's companions, is described as hearing

the Muses in a ring,
Ay round about Jove's altar sing.

(47–8)

And in his *Elegia Sexta*, having playfully alluded to his own 'empty stomach' (*non pleno ventre*) in contrast to his friend Diodati's 'full one', Milton distinguishes between the kinds of poetry each may therefore write, and insists that a frugal life and diet becomes the poet who, intending to embrace more serious themes, seeks to write about 'wars', 'a heaven ruled over by a Jove who has outgrown his boyhood', and 'the holy counsels of the gods above' (*sancta . . . superum consulta deorum*). Apart from *Il Penseroso*, there is perhaps no clearer statement in Milton's early verse of that disciplined regimen to be followed by the poet who aspires to epic and heroic strains. But *Il Penseroso* looks forward to a particular kind of epic poetry. In it the Pythagorean doctrine has been Christianized, and this shift in the poem's framework of reference is indicated by the almost immediate introduction of the 'cherub Contemplation' and the allusion to Ezekiel's prophecy. Later, though it is the seemingly pastoral music of nature that accompanies the 'strange mysterious dream' of poetic inspiration, the implicit suggestion of some meaning more than 'meets the ear' is finally and explicitly confirmed by the richly polyphonic music with a Christian setting that Il Penseroso hopes will take his soul captive through the ear and put him in touch with the divine and eternal:

> But let my due feet never fail,
> To walk the studious cloister's pale . . .
> There let the pealing organ blow,
> To the full-voiced choir below,
> In service high, and anthems clear,
> As may with sweetness, through mine ear,
> Dissolve me into ecstasies,
> And bring all heaven before mine eyes.
>
> (155–6, 161–6)

That Milton later sustained the 'great argument' of *Paradise Lost* clearly indicates which of the two goddesses (or 'Muses') was to preside over his own poetic life. Understandably, it is difficult not to view *Il Penseroso* as reflecting the temperament of its author. Even the final couplet—

> These pleasures Melancholy give,
> And I with thee will choose to live—

arguably sounds a note of convinced commitment not discernible in the more tentative

> These delights, if thou canst give,
> Mirth with thee, I mean to live.

But it is surely mistaken to suggest, as Geckle has done, that the reader of *L'Allegro* finds himself, at the end of the poem, back in the 'Stygian cave forlorn'.[47] Instead the mood is one of 'heaped Elysian flowers'. Such criticism, for all its 'newness', is no more relevant than the autobiographical corollaries of an earlier generation. Of these Dorian has provided an example by suggesting, in effect, that Milton was, when he wrote his companion poems, at the crossroads of his poetic career, and that they represent his attempt to clarify for himself the direction that his future poetry should take. It may in any case be argued that this was a question he had already decided; certainly the inference to be drawn from his *Elegia Sexta*, and from the measured aims expressed in *At a Vacation Exercise*, is clear enough. To me it seems more relevant to suggest that the companion poems' semblance of debate-like structure is reminiscent of the well-established scholastic tradition of disputation, and that in them Milton dedicates himself to enhancing both sides of what is, in an important sense, the same question. Yet what he produces is not argument but poetry, and one can only refer to his 'wit' in terms of a poetic gift that itself suggests the limitations of the traditional distinction which had supplied him with his starting-point. This is not to say that in these poems Milton has written either comedy or tragedy, or, indeed, other examples of the two literary kinds. But his poems do reflect two different kinds of sensibility, and in this respect, at least, may be regarded as giving expression to those two sides of the poetic temperament—represented by L'Allegro and Il Penseroso respectively—which had commonly been thought of as incapable of artistic fulfilment by one and the same man.

Notes

1 'Milton: *L'Allegro* and *Il Penseroso*', *English Association Pamphlets*, No. 82 (1932), p. 7.

2 *Ibid.*, pp. 6, 11ff.

3 *The Well Wrought Urn* (New York, 1947), pp. 53, 59.

4 'Milton's *L'Allegro* and *Il Penseroso*', *The Explicator*, VIII (1950), item 49.

5 'The Place of Music in *L'Allegro* and *Il Penseroso*', *UTQ*, XXII (1953), 365–6.

6 *The Harmonious Vision: Studies in Milton's Poetry* (Baltimore, 1954), esp. pp. 17ff.

7 *Images and Themes in Five Poems by Milton* (Cambridge, Mass., 1957), esp. pp. 20, 26.

8 'Milton's *L'Allegro* and *Il Penseroso*—Balance, Progression, or Dichotomy?', *MLN*, LXXVI (1961), 589.

9 'Miltonic Idealism: *L'Allegro* and *Il Penseroso*', *Texas Studies in Literature and Language*, IX (1968), 455.

10 'The Question of Autobiographical Significance in *L'Allegro* and *Il Penseroso*', *MP*, XXXI (1933), 175, 182.

11 *Poetics*, IV. 8, 13.

12 Cf. F. W. Emerson, 'Why Milton uses "Cambuscan" and "Camball" ', *MLN*, XLVII (1932), 153–4.

13 R. S. Forsythe, '*The Passionate Shepherd* and English Poetry', *PMLA*, XL (1925), 714; Sara R. Watson, 'Milton's Ideal Day: Its Development as a Pastoral Theme', *ibid.*, LVII (1942), 404–20.

14 Cf. Tuve, *Images and Themes in Five Poems by Milton*, p. 18.

15 *The Poems of John Milton*, ed. John Carey and Alastair Fowler (London, 1968), p. 118. In this edition, to which I am indebted for many references and the translation of other Latin phrases, the Latin quoted above is translated as follows: 'But why complain that banquet and bottle frighten poetry away? Song loves Bacchus, and Bacchus loves songs.'

16 I cite this example because, as Carey points out, Jonson had

rhymed 'a Maying' and 'playing' in the song of Aurora, Zephyrus and Flora (ll. 93ff.).

17 Cited by A. H. Gilbert, *The Symbolic Persons in the Masques of Ben Jonson* (New York, 1965 reprint), p. 50.

18 'Milton's Ideal Day: Its Development as a Pastoral Theme', p. 420. (Most of the authors and poems mentioned in the subsequent discussion of this question are cited by Miss Watson.)

19 Cf. *Colin Clouts Come Home Again*, ll. 376ff.

20 George Wither, *The Shepherd's Hunting*, Eclogue V, ll. 151–4.

21 Cf. Spenser's *October* and the fifth Eclogue of Browne's *The Shepherd's Pipe*.

22 *The Shepheard's Garland*, VII. 37–40.

23 See Lawrence Babb, 'The Background of *Il Penseroso*', *SP*, XXXVII (1940), 257–73; Z. S. Fink, '*Il Penseroso*, Line 16', *PQ*, XIX (1940), 309–13; Tuve, pp. 24ff.; R. Klibansky, E. Panofsky and F. Saxl, *Saturn and Melancholy* (London, 1964), esp. pp. 217ff.

24 *Ibid.*, p. 259 and n. 53. Cicero first used the term *furor* (see *Tusculan Disputations*, III. v. 11).

25 *Anatomy of Melancholy*, I. iii. 1. 3; cited by Fink, p. 312.

26 Tuve, pp. 27–8.

27 *Saturn and Melancholy*, pp. 259–60 and nn.

28 Cf. C. G. Osgood, *The Classical Mythology of Milton's English Poems* (New York, 1900), pp. lviiiff.

29 *Saturn and Melancholy*, p. 230.

30 *On Shakespeare*, ll. 13–14.

31 *Saturn and Melancholy*, p. 229.

32 'Milton among the Nightingales', *Renaissance Papers* (1959), pp. 36–45.

33 Tuve, p. 31.

34 Allen, pp. 13–14.

35 *Lives of the Poets*, ed. G. B. Hill (Oxford, 1905), I. 165–6, 167.

36 '*L'Allegro* and *Il Penseroso* in their Relation to Seventeenth Century Poetry', *ESEA*, n.s. IV (1951), 7–9, 15.

37 *Metamorphoses*, XI. 592ff. The allusion is recorded in *John Milton: Complete Poems and Major Prose*, ed. M. Y. Hughes (New York, 1957), p. 68n. Milton's 'ebon' might have been suggested by Ovid's *ebeno* (l. 610).

38 It is interesting, though not conclusive, to note that these lines of *Il Penseroso* recall Night's invoking of Phant'sie in Jonson's *Vision of Delight*, and that Jonson's passage seems in turn to have owed something to Spenser's description of Fancy. Cf. Gilbert, *The Symbolic Persons in the Masques of Ben Jonson*, pp. 193–4.

39 *Complete Prose Works of John Milton*, gen. ed. D. M. Wolfe (New Haven, 1953–), I. 289 and n.1.

40 For examples of dreams that Chaucer attributes to atrabilious melancholy see *Troilus and Criseyde*, V. 358–61, and *The Nun's Priest's Tale*, B 4123–6.
41 'A Poem Nearly Anonymous', in *Milton's 'Lycidas': The Tradition and the Poem*, ed. C. A. Patrides (New York, 1961), pp. 80–1.
42 *Lives of the Poets*, I. 166–7.
43 *5 Pens in Hand* (New York, 1958), pp. 39–41.
44 'The Place of Music in *L'Allegro* and *Il Penseroso*', p. 355.
45 Tuve, p. 24.
46 See Gretchen L. Finney, 'Ecstasy and Music in Seventeenth-Century England', *JHI*, VIII (1947), 153–86.
47 'Miltonic Idealism: *L'Allegro* and *Il Penseroso*', pp. 465, 468.

Lycidas

Modern criticism of *Lycidas* has rightly found unacceptable Dr Johnson's strictures on the 'trifling fictions' of its pastoral imagery and its 'irreverent combinations' of pagan and Christian elements.[1] It is now understood that Milton was using the pastoral convention in the broader spirit of the Renaissance tradition.[2] Yet the precise nature of the poem's structure, which depends on the dual significance of its pastoral imagery, is not, even so, generally understood. Admittedly, a very few critics have discerned what this structure is in broad outline; but none has satisfactorily accounted for the metamorphosis of the pagan shepherds and their grief in terms of the dramatic framework within which this occurs. The result is that critical analysis of the poem has proved to be weak where it should have been most convincing. Not only does this metamorphosis make the final climax of *Lycidas* seem uniquely compelling, but until it is shown how the poem's various elements, pagan and Christian, classical and Scriptural, are finally brought together and reconciled, its unity must arguably remain suspect.

M. H. Abrams, in challenging various modern interpretations of the poem, is surely right to stress that it is 'clearly a dramatic lyric'.[3] Described by its author as a 'monody', *Lycidas* has the rhetorical structure that can be inferred from its last eight lines: 'Thus sang the uncouth swain to the oaks and rills . . .'. Up to this point the poem is the utterance of a single dramatic voice; and except in those passages that contain apparent interruptions by Phoebus and St Peter to the swain's monologue, it clearly implies an audience that hears or overhears his words. This is not just an audience of 'oaks and rills'—though the pathetic fallacy of the pastoral mode imparts to such details of the natural world a special animation. From the poem itself it is clear that, except for the words he addresses to Lycidas himself, the swain addresses the Muses, the resident deities of wood and stream, and the 'woeful shepherds' (ultimately no longer woeful) that inhabit with him the pastoral landscape. (His appeal to St Michael and the 'dolphins' will be mentioned in some detail later.) His assumed audience, then, is primarily that whole pastoral world with classical and pagan associations to which he as poet-shepherd at least initially belongs.

Though John Crowe Ransom, detecting in the poem what he calls 'a breach in the logic of composition', has suggested that in certain places, such as the Phoebus and St Peter passages, 'the narrative breaks the monologue . . . presenting action sometimes in the present tense, sometimes in the past',[4] the words of Phoebus and St Peter are to be regarded not as interruptions to the swain's monologue, but as having been heard only by him, and as recalled at appropriate points of the poem's developing action. As a result of hearing their words, he progressively attains—at least by comparison with the audience that elsewhere hears or overhears his words—the kind of insight or greater knowledge naturally associated with a poet-speaker. In fact, the use of different 'tenses' at these and other points in the poem has been skilfully contrived, serving to reinforce rather than detract from our impression of *Lycidas* as process or performance. As Lowry Nelson Jr has shown in his discussion of baroque lyric poetry, Milton uses a series of 'time planes' (rather than tenses) to create a 'time perspective', bringing the action progressively forward from various times in the past and then consolidating it in the continuing present.[5]

The swain's monologue is obviously dramatic in the very important sense that it moves from a deep and, as it were, pagan despair, to a triumphant affirmation of faith in a Christian resurrection. As Abrams says, 'Milton achieves this . . . by a gradual shift from the natural, pastoral, and pagan viewpoint to the viewpoint of Christian revelation and its promise of another world, the Kingdom of Heaven'.[6] The words of Phoebus and St Peter mark important stages in this movement from despair to triumphant joy. And expressive of this movement is the dual significance of the poem's central imagery. After the swain, who is at first to be identified as a poet-shepherd of classical pastoral, has been made aware of the Christian meaning (including the specifically Christian rewards) of the 'faithful herdman's art' (l. 121), he is in a position to convince his pagan audience of 'woeful shepherds' of this higher Christian truth. Thus the whole poem may be regarded as a therapy of grief dramatized in terms of its pastoral imagery.

So great, however, is the swain's initial despair that he appears to be almost alienated from his pastoral world. What he feels is not just overwhelming grief but a certain uncomprehending anger. His coming to 'shatter' its leaves now that

> Lycidas is dead, dead ere his prime,
> Young Lycidas, and hath not left his peer,
>
> (8–9)

implies something more than the intractableness of his own young muse, or even the premature and unripe nature of the garland he is forced to pluck for his departed friend. The explosive violence of his act mirrors an intransigence that results not only from his unwillingness to accept the fact of premature death, but also from a certain questioning of the pastoral world itself. In what is arguably a reflection of the desolation that he himself feels—a desolation that contrasts sharply with his expression of a 'genuine emotion about Nature"[7] as he recalls the pleasures that, as a young poet-shepherd, he shared with his friend—the pastoral world seems not only grief-stricken but blighted. And since this world is a figure for the poetic vocation itself, the swain is in the paradoxical position of having to affirm that 'some melodious tear' (l. 14) is Lycidas's due even as he questions whether it took proper care of its beloved shepherd. The 'bitter constraint' he experiences now that Lycidas is 'gone' (l. 37) is barely contained by the convention. The 'sisters of the sacred well' (l. 15) are not so much invoked as bidden to attend, the possibility even being implied that the swain himself could die without receiving in his turn a fitting poetic tribute. Moreover, in his address to the nymphs who inhabit this world as resident deities, and who are therefore fittingly linked with its 'old bards, the famous Druids', there can be heard a note of almost peremptory questioning absent from those passages of classical pastoral which these lines have been taken to echo:

> Where were ye nymphs when the remorseless deep
> Closed o'er the head of your loved Lycidas?
> For neither were ye playing on the steep . . .
> Nor . . .
>
> (50ff.)

The underlying tension between the swain and his pastoral world is, in fact, increased, not dispelled, by the apparent disclaimer that follows, for the example of Orpheus only serves to emphasize even more strongly a sense of the inherent futility of the poetic vocation.

It is the poet-shepherd's dedication to this vocation that is explicitly questioned in the swain's next words, which, together with Phoebus's reply, constitute the poem's first climax. Since even the Muse herself could not save her 'enchanting son' (l. 59), why 'strictly meditate the thankless muse?' (l. 66). For the poet-shepherd there is apparently no protection against the ravages of the 'blind Fury' (l. 75). And so the swain questions whether the pastoral life as he knows it is not pointless:

31

Were it not better done as others use,
To sport with Amaryllis in the shade,
Or with the tangles of Neaera's hair?

(67–9)

With these lines we suddenly become aware of a choice of life
that, existing even within the pastoral world, gives added point to
the swain's questioning.

The answer returned by Phoebus contains a line,

Phoebus replied, and touched my trembling ears,

(77)

that directly echoes Virgil's *Cynthius aurem/vellit et admonuit*.[8] As
the Virgilian context makes clear, the Roman poet-shepherd had
been warned not to sing epic strains, but instead to feed *pinguis
ovis* ('fat sheep') and sing *deductum carmen* ('a fine-spun lay'). Milton's Phoebus, however, makes no distinction unfavourable to
poetry of a more serious kind; instead one might assume that this
would be the very poetry—the product of a more dedicated commitment—to receive his unqualified approval. Yet the Virgilian
allusion is at least suggestive of the swain's coming reconciliation,
as poet, with the pastoral world: on receiving Phoebus's assurance
that a higher power guarantees the immortality of the dedicated
poet-shepherd's fame, he significantly modifies his sense of out-
rage. Since the gods unfailingly recognize the merit inherent in all
noble striving, it is implied that even Lycidas, 'dead ere his prime',
will enjoy, in this sense at least, his due reward in 'heaven'.

It is for this reason that I find unacceptable David Daiches'
suggestion that the next verse-paragraph 'ends on a note of frustration and even despair'.[9] This section of the poem, with its
return to the prevailing mode, reflects an important stage in the
metamorphosis of the swain's grief. No longer does he hold the
pastoral world (now in some sense vindicated by the gods above)
responsible for Lycidas's death. Mincius is fittingly addressed as
'thou honoured flood/ . . . crowned with vocal reeds'. And the

questioning that follows is something from which the swain himself stands apart. He 'listens' as

> the herald of the sea
> That came in Neptune's plea
>
> (89–90)

interrogates with an impartial and impressive dignity the 'felon
winds'—where 'felon' means no more than 'savage' or 'wild', as in
the French phrase *de vents felons* that obviously inspired Milton's.[10]
Nor are we surprised to find when

> sage Hippotades their answer brings,
> That not a blast was from his dungeon strayed,
> The air was calm, and on the level brine,
> Sleek Panope with all her sisters played.
>
> (96–9)

The swain's initial anger and frustration now appropriately find
an outlet only in his angry denunciation of 'the perfidious bark'—
and for this the pagan deities cannot themselves be blamed. His
grief has, however, only been partially metamorphosed; Phoebus
can offer only a limited consolation. The reward held out to the
'clear spirit' (l. 70) does not, as has been erroneously suggested,
bring with it 'the Christian assurance of immortality'.[11] If Phoebus
had delivered St Peter's message, there would have been no need
for the latter to appear.

The St Peter passage has especially troubled critics of *Lycidas*. To
some it has seemed an unwarrantable, if characteristic, digression.
Ransom, for example, detects in it 'a Milton who is angry, violent,
and perhaps a little bit vulgar'.[12] But far from being an ill-con-
trived interruption of the pastoral mode, this passage significantly
increases the resonance of Milton's central imagery. By enabling

33

the swain to comprehend the meaning of the Christian 'pastoral' vocation, it creates a gap in awareness between him and his pagan audience. And since the way in which *Lycidas* moves to its final and climatic resolution is directly related to this gap in awareness, the St Peter passage is obviously essential to the dramatic structure of the poem.

Yet the large majority of the poem's recent critics have interpreted St Peter's message as even less optimistic than Phoebus's. According to Cleanth Brooks and John Edward Hardy, '. . . if St Peter's speech, like Apollo's, transcends the pastoral mode, it carries us away from the hope that Apollo's words had suggested'.[13] The terms in which critics have compared the poem's first two climaxes may be illustrated by the following quotations:

Both passages end with a promise of final judgment. The chief difference between the two promises is that St Peter assures only the punishment of the wicked; Apollo, only the reward of the good.[14]

The god who calms the first wave of doubt is the god of justice and emphasis is laid on his impartiality, his 'perfect witness'. . . . The god of the second part is the apocalyptic god of retribution, whose single blow is sufficient to crush the armies of the godless . . . To quote the language of another poem, it is the 'rigid satisfaction, Death for Death,' which has dominated the first two 'resolutions' in *Lycidas*.[15]

The two episodes, presided over by the figures of Orpheus [*sic*] and Peter, deal with the theme of premature death as it relates to poetry and to the priesthood respectively. In both the same type of image appears: the mechanical instrument of execution that brings about a sudden death, represented by the 'abhorred shears' in the meditation on fame and the 'grim two-handed engine' in the meditation on the corruption of the Church.[16]

A reader of this last quotation might well be forgiven were he to assume that the 'two-handed engine' has already been used to smite Lycidas himself! Even Abrams, who not only stresses that the poem has a rhetorical structure, but realizes that through the Christian parallels of this passage 'the resolution of the elegy is assured', surprisingly concludes:

> The elegiac singer . . . is momentarily occupied with the specific references rather than the Scriptural overtones of Peter's comment, with the result that the resolution, so skilfully planted in his evolving thought, is delayed until he has tried to interpose a little ease by strewing imaginary flowers on Lycidas' imagined hearse.

In accordance with the usual view, Abrams locates the 'point of profoundest depression' immediately prior to the poem's climactic resolution.[17] Thus my disagreement with critics over the St Peter passage will perforce become a continuing disagreement. Obviously the significance one attributes to this passage inevitably determines how one reads much of the rest of the poem.

Coming last in the procession of mourners, St Peter bears a message of spiritual life as well as the threat of damnation:[18]

> Last came, and last did go,
> The pilot of the Galilean lake,
> Two massy keys he bore of metals twain,
> (The golden opes, the iron shuts amain).
>
> (108–11)

Whether these keys are meant to recall those that Christ gave Peter in Matthew, XVI. 19, or those 'keys of hell and of death' that Christ is himself represented as carrying in Revelation, I. 18, it is obvious, as Michael Lloyd has pointed out, that Milton is here setting 'heaven against hell, the golden against the iron'.[19] These are the metals used to describe the gates of heaven and hell in *Paradise Lost*: whereas the 'gate' (or 'gates') of heaven 'self-opened wide/On golden hinges turning' (V. 254-5, VII. 205-8), the gate of hell had bolts and bars 'of massy iron or solid rock'

(II, 877-8)

(II. 877–8). Moreover, though it has recently been claimed (in accordance with the usual interpretation of the passage) that St Peter's speech 'offers nothing to assuage grief for the loss of Lycidas, and nothing to suggest any ultimate justice for him personally',[20] an emphatic distinction is surely made between Lycidas and those other 'shepherds' who have so completely abnegated their proper pastoral responsibility of caring for God's flock. These are fittingly described as

> Blind mouths! that scarce themselves know how to hold
> A sheep-hook, or have learned aught else the least
> That to the faithful herdman's art belongs!
>
> (119–21)

Indeed, St Peter's denunciation of the corrupt clergy makes plain his very different assessment of Lycidas's brief but exemplary service in the pastoral tradition begun by Christ himself. And the clear implication of this—an implication reinforced by the echoes of Christ's own pastoral parable in this passage[21]—is that Lycidas's ultimate fate cannot be equated with theirs. Thus St Peter provides an implicit answer to Camus's previous exclamation of grief: 'Ah; who hath reft (quoth he) my dearest pledge?' (l. 107). As the poem goes on to illustrate, it is Christ himself who will redeem the life of this 'good shepherd'.[22]

That this message can be inferred from St Peter's words is evident from the reference to the 'door' in the concluding lines:

> But that two-handed engine at the door,
> Stands ready to smite once, and smite no more.
>
> (130–1)

This is a figure for Christ himself, as John, X. 9 makes clear: 'I am the door: by me if any man enter in, he shall be saved, and shall go in and out, and find pasture'. Through this 'door' the faithful will enter the Kingdom of Heaven; and that Lycidas will be of their number is guaranteed by this whole passage and St Peter's presence as a mourner. Thus the troublesome 'But' of line 130 may be

36

taken as adversative even to the first words St Peter utters: the 'young swain' Lycidas will ultimately be 'spared' in the all-important sense that he will enjoy everlasting life.

'But' is also, of course, clearly adversative to the rest of St Peter's speech, the implication being that the false 'shepherds', as well as the 'grim wolf' of Catholicism, will, unlike Lycidas, be prevented from entering the fold of the faithful, the Kingdom of Heaven. The 'two-handed engine' is most usually interpreted as a symbol of the Word of God, which is described in Revelation, I. 16 as 'a sharp twoedged sword', in Hebrews, IV. 12 as 'quick, and powerful, and sharper than any twoedged sword', and had once been represented in the device of the Geneva printer Jehan Gerard as a two-handed broadsword, in order to suggest its active power in the Protestant Reformation.[23] Thus Milton's 'two-handed engine' has been identified with 'the power of the Protestant Reformation which substituted the authority of the Bible for that of the Church and was being carried to its logical conclusion in the Puritan movement of his own day'.[24] Yet also consonant with the context in which it occurs is its interpretation as a symbol of the Word of God that will make itself manifest at the final Judgment by smiting its enemies once and for all. In both Hebrews, IV. 12 and Revelation, I. 16, the 'twoedged sword' is mentioned in a context implying Divine Judgment. And the latter passage looks forward to the description of God's Judgment later in the same Book, where it is said that 'out of his mouth goeth a sharp sword, that with it he should smite the nations' (XIX. 15). Moreover, even if Milton's 'two-handed engine' is, as some critics have variously claimed, to be identified either with the sword of Divine Justice (Ezekiel, XXI. 9ff.), especially as wielded by Michael 'with huge two-handed sway' (*Paradise Lost*, VI. 251), or with 'Christ's rod, the instrument of divine justice',[25] there is obviously present the same idea of a Divine Judgment at which the ungodly shall be separated from the righteous.

The climactic lines of the St Peter passage may therefore be regarded as balancing the climactic lines of the Phoebus passage only in the sense that both of these passages conclude with a reference to a supernatural judgment. As we might anyway have expected, the second climax of the poem more nearly anticipates the final climax because it provides a specific assurance of that Christian Judgment which involves not only damnation but salvation.

The swain, enlightened as a result of overhearing St Peter's words, is now in a position to comfort and instruct a pagan world still grieving for its dead Lycidas. This is the dramatic situation attendant on the return to the pastoral mode; yet this has, even so, received little relevant attention from critics of the poem. According to Wayne Shumaker, whose commentary on the next verse-paragraph is certainly the most detailed and perhaps the best known, the celebrated catalogue of flowers, of which 'the notion is too pretty-pretty, too conventionally poetic to carry a heavy emotional weight', is followed by a mood of 'profound spiritual depression' that passes 'by a natural emotional rhythm . . . into the final rapture'.[26] Even Abrams, who has a more accurate sense of the poem's rhetorical structure, concentrates so exclusively on the 'evolving meditation of the speaker himself' that he shows no awareness of the presence of a pagan audience that as yet lacks knowledge of Christian resurrection.[27] That such an audience is implied is clear both from the use of 'our' in lines 153 and 159, and from the swain's later apostrophe to the 'woeful shepherds'. Moreover, as might anyway have been expected in the work of a poet who considered decorum as 'the grand master peece to observe',[28] Milton exploits this dramatic situation with a nice sense of the respective fictional roles of the swain and his audience. The former, who has been enlightened by overhearing St Peter's words, appropriately confines himself to such examples and allusions as will be readily comprehensible to a pagan audience that has still to be made aware of Lycidas's resurrection.

The celebrated catalogue of flowers is not, as Daiches suggests, Milton's attempt 'to transmute the dead Lycidas into something beautiful and fragrant'—a sort of 'apology', or making 'amends' to him, 'for having to forsake him at the last'.[29] Nor is it, as Brooks and Hardy suggest, ironic, indicating that 'nature is neutral', that 'it does not participate in grief for the dead man'.[30] Instead it constitutes the first stage of a final movement towards the poem's climactic resolution, providing, together with the later water imagery, also symbolic of resurrection, a remarkable enactment of the therapy of grief.

Though the first draft of the poem did not include the catalogue of individual flowers, it did contain the following reference to the floral freshness of spring:

> Ye valleys low where the mild whispers use . . .
> Throw hither all your quaint enamelled eyes,
> That on the green turf suck the honied showers,
> And purple all the ground with vernal flowers.

(136ff.)

These lines might have been meant to recall that Lycidas died 'ere his prime', or to indicate the resurgence of hope and reawakened feeling on the part of the swain now that he knows there is no cause for immoderate grieving. Yet Milton's additional lines are especially significant in that they allow the swain to begin to prepare a grieving pagan world ultimately to accept the joyous truth of Lycidas's resurrection. The catalogue of flowers, in which each flower is so wonderfully evoked as to seem an individualized presence, represents an invitation to this world to rouse itself from its formerly inert and blighted state by taking part in an elaborate ritual of mourning. The use of pathetic fallacy is here so deft that the individual flowers seem to be individual mourners in a continuous funeral procession.[31]

Unless the reader is at this point expressly conscious of the presence of a pagan audience, he will be unaware of what provides the moment of greatest tension in this whole therapy of grief. Though a funeral without a body seems always to arouse a vague sense of dismay, in classical times an unburied corpse was a cause of considerable anguish. So well known was this to Milton's original audience that the swain's 'false surmise' (l. 153) would have been understood as administering a shock of horror to his pagan audience of classical shepherds. As Virgil's description of Aeneas's visit to the underworld makes clear, the unburied dead were thought of as wandering sad and homeless for a hundred years before they could be carried to their longed-for resting-place. The catalogue of flowers thus brings together the pagan world's moment of deepest anguish and its ritual of unrivalled beauty. To describe this as 'too pretty-pretty, too conventionally poetic to carry a heavy emotional weight', is to miss the point of its psychological significance. The 'little ease' that the swain seeks 'to interpose' by means of this ritual is ultimately not ironic, but has a very real effect: the pagan world is compelled to acknowledge the ultimate depths of its sorrow even as it is compelled, in some degree, to master it.

Since the body of Lycidas has been lost at sea, the imaginary strewing of his hearse with flowers makes possible a felicitous transition to the all-important water imagery. This both allows the facts of his death to be vividly recalled, and looks forward to the exemplum on which the final resolution turns. Far from reflecting a mood of 'profound spiritual depression', the 'sounding seas' passage, the most sonorous in the poem, continues the process by which the grief of the pagan world is sublimated:

> Ay me! Whilst thee the shores, and sounding seas
> Wash far away, where'er thy bones are hurled,
> Whether beyond the stormy Hebrides
> Where thou perhaps under the whelming tide
> Visit'st the bottom of the monstrous world;
> Or whether thou to our moist vows denied,
> Sleep'st by the fable of Bellerus old,
> Where the great vision of the guarded mount
> Looks toward Namancos and Bayona's hold;
> Look homeward angel now, and melt with ruth.
> And, O ye dolphins, waft the hapless youth.

> (154-64)

Miss Tuve remarks that 'the irony in the intimate communication in "visit'st" is less grim than piteous'.[32] But there is surely a fur-

ther sense in which this 'intimate communication' is almost
volitional, serving to invest Lycidas's corpse with quasi-heroic
associations. The 'moist vows' of the pagan mourners are 'denied'
because Lycidas 'sleeps' by the shores that commemorate his
country's legendary ancestors. As Daiches remarks:

> To see Lycidas in this context is to see him in conjunction
> with English history and with the guardian angel of England,
> St Michael, who looks out over the sea towards the long-
> since-defeated Spanish enemy. He [i.e. Milton] has thus at last
> managed to associate Lycidas with a sense of triumph.[33]

The pagan world becomes the more readily reconciled to its loss
because Lycidas has suffered a fate greater than death. Even though
it has yet to be revealed that he becomes 'the genius of the shore'
(l. 183), the final appeal to St Michael and the dolphins is clearly
made from a consciousness of what the lost poet-shepherd symbolizes. Here it is relevant to remember the example of Orpheus,
whose head had brought to Lesbos (cf. l. 63) the divine gift of
poetry, and whose story had commonly been interpreted as an al-
legory of the shifting cycles of civilization and barbarism. Thus
the appeal to St Michael and the dolphins to 'look homeward' and
'waft the hapless youth' reflects a desire to have poetry, learning
and civilization preserved within England itself.[34] Nor would the
significance of this reference to the dolphins have been lost on an
audience familiar with the stories of Arion, Icadius and Palaemon
(the last of whom became, like Lycidas himself, a patron of marin-
ers).[35] As Miss Tuve asserts, 'both the echo of Orpheus, and
Arion's winning harmonies that won the dolphin's love, are too
valuable for Milton to forego them'. So richly suggestive is the
imagery of these lines that the reader seems meant to recall that
the dolphin was a symbol both of the Resurrection and (though
more rarely) of Christ himself. Again Miss Tuve points out that
'the love and rescuing pity which had long been thought of as the
beauty of Arion's story are like in character to the saving heavenly
Love that walk'd the waves'.[36]

.   .   .

In one sense, then, the reference to the dolphins may be regarded as anticipating the reference to Lycidas's resurrection in the next, climactic verse-paragraph.

> Weep no more, woeful shepherds weep no more,
> For Lycidas your sorrow is not dead,
> Sunk though he be beneath the watery floor,
> So sinks the day-star in the ocean bed,
> And yet anon repairs his drooping head,
> And tricks his beams, and with new spangled ore,
> Flames in the forehead of the morning sky:
> So Lycidas sunk low, but mounted high,
> Through the dear might of him that walked the waves.
>
> (165–73)

The explanation of this climactic resolution in terms of Milton's frequent use, throughout the poem, of imagery symbolic of rebirth has, in fact, hitherto seemed more convincing than such explanations as have been based on an analysis of the poem's affective or rhetorical structure. Shumaker, for example, in order to explain the transition to 'ecstatic and thrilling joy', postulates 'a natural emotional rhythm, illustrated on the abnormal level by the familiar manic-depressive pattern'.[37] And Abrams, though he rightly acknowledges that the St Peter passage carries an assurance of Lycidas's final resurrection, has to assume a slow-witted swain who only realizes 'the full implication of St Peter's speech' as he comes to think 'of Lycidas' body sinking to "the bottom of the monstrous world" '.[38] Yet while no one would deny the force and suggestiveness of Milton's symbolic imagery, the critical attention lavished on this has tended to obscure the poem's sharpness of dramatic outline. What is needed is an explanation of this climactic resolution (where the pagan and Christian elements are finally brought together and reconciled) that does not detract from our impression of the poem as process or performance. Thus, in order to preserve the nature of the experience that *Lycidas* so uniquely embodies, the critic must first of all be able to explain the final climax in terms of the dramatic situation that obtains at precisely this point in the poem's developing action.

When, however, we turn to those critics who have rightly acknowledged the poem's inherently dramatic structure, we find that they have really only begged the question. William G. Madsen, for example, suggests that the 'woeful shepherds' are addressed not by the swain but by St Michael:[39]

> How can the person who plaintively and ineffectually calls on the dolphins to waft the hapless youth suddenly speak with the unambiguous accents of authority? The answer is that he cannot. The current confusion about *Lycidas*, I suggest, has resulted from assuming that the consolation is spoken by the uncouth swain. We have failed to hear the voice of Michael.

What Madsen does not, however, explain, in assuming that the swain is still a pagan figure, is why he should have been convinced by St Michael if he were not convinced by St Peter. Lowry Nelson, on the other hand, though more nearly aware of the change in the speaker's role, undercuts the pastoral imagery in the opposite direction:[40]

> At the beginning of the third section, the mourners addressed for the first time are those who, together with the speaker, were fictionally closest to Lycidas, namely the shepherds (poets or clerics):
>
> > Weep no more, woeful shepherds weep no more,
> > For Lycidas your sorrow is not dead . . .

It is therefore necessary to insist that the 'woeful shepherds' are weeping because up to this point they are still represented as pagans. They have yet to learn that their grief is unnecessary, that Lycidas has risen from a death that to them had seemed final. To regard them all along as Christians only succeeds in robbing the situation of its dramatic immediacy, and the climax of the poem of its special force.

In a way that is peculiarly appropriate to its dramatic context, Milton's climactic verse-paragraph makes use of that well-established literary topos which had depicted primitive man as inconsolable when he saw the first sun set. This topos is found in Manilius:[41]

> Nam rudis ante illos, nullo discrimine, vita
> In speciem conversa, operum ratione carebat,
> Et stupefacta novo pendebat lumine mundi;
> Tum velut amissis moerens, tum laeta renatis
> Sideribus . . .

It is also found in Statius:[42]

> Hi [i.e. Arcades] lucis stupuisse vices, noctisque feruntur
> Nubila, et occiduum longe Titana secuti
> Desperasse diem.

And it was mocked at by Lucretius in describing the behaviour of men during earth's infancy.[43] In English literature it was to be used again by Marvell in his *First Anniversary of the Government under O.C.*[44] And it was later used by Johnson in *Rasselas*, where Imlac likens 'the state of a mind oppressed with a sudden calamity' to 'that of the fabulous inhabitants of the new-created earth, who, when the first night came upon them, supposed that day never would return'.[45] Milton's 'woeful shepherds', like primitive man, have experienced an overwhelming grief in losing the light of their world; yet they are sophisticated enough to know (like Lucretius's primitive men, who had experienced the same phenomenon many times before) that the sun will rise again. The swain's exemplum would naturally have impressed itself vividly on their consciousness because, as shepherds, their whole life was regulated by the sun. Yet this image possesses a further dramatic propriety in that it serves to underline the gap in awareness between the swain and his audience. Compared to the greater knowledge that he now has, his audience of 'woeful shepherds' is indeed little more than a group of primitive men. He himself is able not only to assert

Lycidas's resurrection by drawing on a vivid analogy from the natural world, but to account for it in explicitly Christian terms:

> So Lycidas sunk low, but mounted high,
> Through the dear might of him that walked the waves . . .

By what may be regarded as at least an apt poetic logic, the pagan shepherds are metamorphosed along with their grief. The whole landscape of classical pastoral receives its final apotheosis in those 'other groves' (l. 174) that are perhaps intended to recall the description of 'the tree of life' in Revelation, XXII. 2, and in those 'other streams' that recall the 'living fountains of waters' where 'God shall wipe all tears from their eyes' (*ibid.*, VII. 17). Yet the most striking reappearance of the water imagery in this climactic verse-paragraph is, of course, in those lines that explicitly recall that episode in the life of Christ when he not only saved 'the pilot of the Galilean lake', but prefigured the salvation of all the faithful. It is from this higher Christian truth that the final consolation proceeds: the shepherds 'weep no more' (l. 182) because the prince of shepherds has wiped the tears for ever from Lycidas's eyes.

Because of the poem's progression from deep despair at Lycidas's death to triumphant joyousness at his inevitable resurrection, it would seem peculiarly appropriate that it should have stood last in the volume of memorial verses inspired by Edward King's death; indeed, given that the first poem in this volume had contained 'a statement of death as God's punishment of sin',[46] *Lycidas* must have provided its original readers with an appropriate reassurance. Yet since it is a poem about a poet-shepherd rather than just Edward King, it ultimately offers an important reassurance concerning the poet-shepherd's chosen vocation. Milton's use of the pastoral convention may serve to remind us that he regarded the poetic vocation as just as important as the priestly.

45

Within a few years he was to make the point emphatically in one of the most ringing passages of his prose,[47] where he claims that the 'abilities' of the true poet are

> the inspired guift of God rarely bestow'd . . . and are of power beside the office of a pulpit, to inbreed and cherish in a great people the seeds of vertu, and publick civility, to allay the perturbations of the mind, and set the affections in right tune, to celebrate in glorious and lofty Hymns the throne and equipage of Gods Almightinesse, and what he works, and what he suffers to be wrought with high providence in his Church . . .

In the poem itself, Phoebus significantly appears alongside St Peter. When the swain questions the poetic vocation, he does so in response to a seemingly blind and malignant fate that apparently holds out no promise to those dedicated to this higher calling. And that this calling may imply a priestly function is suggested not only by the swain's address to the nymphs and its reference to the Druidic bards, but also by the example of Orpheus, who was himself both poet and priest. Moreover, even after St Peter has made explicit the duties and rewards of the dedicated 'shepherd', this higher Christian calling is conceived in terms that do not exclude the poetic vocation. In the apotheosized pastoral world of the climactic verse-paragraph, the resurrected poet-shepherd, now translated to 'other groves, and other streams',

> hears the unexpressive nuptial song,
> In the blest kingdoms meek of joy and love.
>
> (176–7)

The antithesis of this 'nuptial song', as well as of the poetic vocation itself, is clearly that impulse towards earthly, transitory things represented by Amaryllis and Neaera. And that the resurrected Lycidas 'hears' it—and presumably is to become a member of the 'sweet societies' that sing it—provides an assurance for every poet-shepherd who ever doubted the ultimate fulfilment of his vocation.

This assurance is reinforced by the way in which the pastoral convention is sustained to the very end of the poem. Since the concluding lines present an epitome of the swain's role as poet-speaker, they effectively mask Milton's own identity by tending to confirm the reader's impression of the swain's authenticity. Consequently, though it is perhaps inevitable that the reference in the last line to 'pastures new' will always remind readers of Milton's own poetic aspirations and career, it should be noted that these words have a significance consistent with the context in which they occur. For the swain himself they mark not only an ending but a beginning. In them is heard an echo of those 'other groves, and other streams' that are to influence his pursuit of his chosen vocation. Hopefully they will also witness his own apotheosis.

Notes

1 *Lives of the Poets*, ed. Hill, I. 163–5.
2 Cf. James H. Hanford, 'The Pastoral Elegy and Milton's *Lycidas*', in *Milton's 'Lycidas'*, ed. Patrides, pp. 27–55.
3 'Five Types of *Lycidas*', *ibid.*, p. 222.
4 'A Poem Nearly Anonymous', *ibid.*, p. 79.
5 *Baroque Lyric Poetry* (New Haven & London, 1961), pp. 64ff.
6 'Five Types of *Lycidas*', in *Milton's 'Lycidas'*, pp. 226–7.
7 David Daiches, *ibid.*, p. 107.
8 *Eclogues*, VI. 3–4.
9 In *Milton's 'Lycidas'*, p. 112.
10 Cf. T. P. Harrison, Jr, 'A Note on *Lycidas*, 91', *University of Texas Bulletin: Studies in English*, XV (1935), 22, who points out that de Baïf's *Eclogue* XV contains this phrase in 'association with Neptune and his waves'.
11 J. Milton French, 'The Digressions in Milton's *Lycidas*', *SP*, L (1953), 489. Cf. Marjorie Hope Nicolson, *John Milton: A Reader's Guide to his Poetry* (London, 1964), pp. 95–6 and n.
12 'A Poem Nearly Anonymous', in *Milton's 'Lycidas'*, p. 78.
13 'Essays in Analysis: *Lycidas*', *ibid.*, p. 148.
14 John Edward Hardy, 'Reconsiderations: I. *Lycidas*', *Kenyon Review*, VII (1945), 109.

15 B. Rajan, '*Lycidas*: The Shattering of the Leaves', *SP*, LXIV (1967), 61.

16 Northrop Frye, 'Literature as Context: Milton's *Lycidas*', in *Milton's 'Lycidas'*, p. 202.

17 'Five Types of *Lycidas*', *ibid.*, pp. 228–9.

18 Ralph E. Hone, 'The Pilot of the *Galilean* Lake', *SP*, LVI (1959), 55–61, argues that this figure is intended to represent Christ. Though the usual interpretation seems preferable, it should, perhaps, be pointed out that, according to Hone's interpretation, 'the keys are to be taken as a powerful symbol of the resurrection theme' (p. 59).

19 'The Two Worlds of *Lycidas*', *Essays in Criticism*, XI (1961), 395.

20 John Reesing, *Milton's Poetic Art* (Cambridge, Mass., 1968), p. 22.

21 Cf. Abrams, 'Five Types of *Lycidas*', in *Milton's 'Lycidas'*, p. 228.

22 Cf. Lloyd, 'The Two Worlds of *Lycidas*', pp. 390–1.

23 For a bibliography and summary of interpretations of this famous crux see *ibid.*, pp. 240–1. Cf. esp. Leon Howard, ' "That Two-Handed Engine" Once More', *Huntingdon Library Quarterly*, XV (1952), 173–84; John M. Steadman, 'Milton's "Two-Handed Engine" and Jehan Gerard', *NQ*, CCI (1956), 249–50.

24 Howard, ' "That Two-Handed Engine" Once More', p. 183.

25 Reesing, *Milton's Poetic Art*, pp. 33–4.

26 'Flowerets and Sounding Seas: A Study in the Affective Structure of *Lycidas*', in *Milton's 'Lycidas'*, p. 127.

27 'Five Types of *Lycidas*', *ibid.*, pp. 225, 229.

28 *Complete Prose Works of John Milton*, II. 405.

29 Daiches, in *Milton's 'Lycidas'*, pp. 115–16.

30 'Essays in Analysis: *Lycidas*', *ibid.*, p. 149.

31 Cf. Rajan, '*Lycidas*: The Shattering of the Leaves', p. 54.

32 'Theme, Pattern, and Imagery in *Lycidas*', in *Milton's 'Lycidas'*, p. 187.

33 Daiches, *ibid.*, p. 117.

34 Cf. Caroline W. Mayerson, 'The Orpheus Image in *Lycidas*', *PMLA*, LXIV (1949), 206.

35 Cf. Michael Lloyd, 'The Fatal Bark', *MLN*, LXXV (1960), 105ff.

36 'Theme, Pattern, and Imagery in *Lycidas*', in *Milton's 'Lycidas'*, p. 187 and n. 11.

37 'Flowerets and Sounding Seas: A Study in the Affective Structure of *Lycidas*', *ibid.*, p. 127.

38 'Five Types of *Lycidas*', *ibid.*, p. 229.

39 'The Voice of Michael in *Lycidas*', *Studies in English Literature*, III (1963), 4.

40 *Baroque Lyric Poetry*, pp. 147–8.

41 *Astronomicon*, I. 66–70. ('For prior to those men, primitive life,

looking without distinction at appearance, missed the reality of what was happening, and in horror hung upon the new light of the world, at one time grieving as though the heavenly bodies [sun] were lost, and then rejoicing at their [its] reappearance.')

42 *Thebaid*, IV. 282–4. ('These Arcadians are said to have been astonished at the changes in the day and at the darkness of night, and as they followed the dying Titan from afar off [or for a long while] to have despaired of the day.')

43 *De Rerum Natura*, V. 973ff.

44 Ll. 324ff. Marvell might have been influenced by Milton's earlier use of this topos. At any rate, his phrase 'beaked promontories' (l. 358) seems to be an echo of 'beaked promontory' in line 94 of *Lycidas*.

45 *The History of Rasselas, Prince of Abisinnia*, ed. J. P. Hardy (London, 1968), pp. 85, 167n.

46 Lloyd, 'The Fatal Bark', pp. 107–8.

47 *Complete Prose Works of John Milton*, I. 816–17.

The Rape of the Lock

The Rape of the Lock is currently regarded as presenting a satiric
portrait of its beautiful heroine. In the opinion of most critics
Belinda is a coquette; while Hugo M. Reichard underlines the
point by maintaining that she is 'an invincible flirt'. Reichard ac-
cepts that the love story which seems to lie behind the poem is 'so
obscure as to defy analysis';[1] and certainly the full significance of
the incident that was its immediate occasion (or rather, the occasion of the two-canto version of 1712) can never be precisely
known. Even if it were, our interpretation of Belinda's character
would have to proceed from the text itself—and it is on the text of
the five-canto version that this would have to be based. Nothing
that we might know of Arabella Fermor's conduct in real life, or
of Lord Petre's attitude towards her, could determine, of itself,
our reading of the poem. Yet it may, I believe, be suggested that
this text, because of its inherent and even studied ambiguity,
admits the possibility of a different interpretation of Belinda. And
if this is so, it may further be considered whether such an interpretation of Pope's heroine can be more readily related to the known
facts of the situation that had prompted his friend John Caryll to
ask him to write the poem in the first place.

·   ·   ·

Those who regard Belinda as a coquette accept what Ariel reveals
to her in a dream as a true estimate of her character:

> The light Coquettes in *Sylphs* aloft repair,
> And sport and flutter in the Fields of Air.
>   Know farther yet; Whoever fair and chaste
> Rejects Mankind, is by some *Sylph* embrac'd;
>
> (I. 65–8)

>   Some Nymphs there are, too conscious of their Face,
> For Life predestin'd to the *Gnomes'* Embrace.
> These swell their Prospects and exalt their Pride,
> When Offers are disdain'd, and Love deny'd . . .
>
> (I. 79–82)

Yet despite the fact that Belinda's actions are apparently influenced, first by the sylph Ariel, and later by the gnome Umbriel,
the poem's obliquely stated love-interest would seem to disprove
that Pope's heroine, coquette-like, denies the claims of 'Love'.
Critics who maintain otherwise are in danger of adopting a position which even Ariel himself was forced to abandon when, at the
moment of truth just prior to the 'rape',

> Sudden he view'd, in spite of all her Art,
> An Earthly Lover lurking at her Heart.
>
> (III. 143–4)

These lines arguably indicate that Belinda, who outwardly seems
such a coquette, is nevertheless quite willing to entertain the idea
of an 'earthly lover'. Nor should it be assumed, as has recently been
suggested, that 'she is at that age when she thinks she hates the
boys and cannot understand what is really troubling her'.[2] Con-
sidering the conscious sophistication she so clearly displays, it
would seem rather that Ariel has previously been deceived by her
'art' into mistaking her real motives.

It is, however, what happens in the crucial fifth canto that provides the clearest justification for offering a reinterpretation of

Belinda's character. According to Geoffrey Tillotson, the Twickenham editor, 'Belinda is represented in the poem as meditating
love, as ready indeed to love the Baron, though she unaccountably
rejects him'.[3] And in the words of Aubrey Williams, it is in her
unwillingness to hearken to Clarissa's words that 'she ratifies the
course of prudery delineated earlier in the Cave of Spleen episode,
and persists in the ways of Ill-Nature and Affectation'. 'This',
Williams concludes, 'is her real fall in the poem, and in this the
richest and fairest of the poem's many vessels is irreparably
shattered'.[4] Both Tillotson and Williams obviously have in mind
Belinda's virago-like behaviour during the mêlée that follows
Clarissa's speech. Yet her attitude in this undisguised battle between the sexes has clearly been determined by the outcome of the
previous scene between herself and the Baron, when she does not
so much reject him as suffer rejection at his hands.

   A striking use of anaphora, parallelism and juxtaposition at the
beginning of canto IV wittily suggests, with playful seriousness,
Belinda's justifiably complex reaction to the 'rape':

> But anxious Cares the pensive Nymph opprest,
> And secret Passions labour'd in her Breast.
> Not youthful Kings in Battel seiz'd alive,
> Not scornful Virgins who their Charms survive,
> Not ardent Lovers robb'd of all their Bliss,
> Not ancient Ladies when refus'd a Kiss,
> Not Tyrants fierce that unrepenting die,
> Not *Cynthia* when her *Manteau*'s pinn'd awry,
> E'er felt such Rage, Resentment and Despair,
> As Thou, sad Virgin! for thy ravish'd Hair.

And this reaction is further reflected in the speech she makes after
Umbriel's 'vial' has been broken. Here her dramatized rejection of
the world of society—

> Happy! ah ten times happy, had I been,
> If *Hampton-Court* these Eyes had never seen!
> Yet am I not the first mistaken Maid,

By Love of *Courts* to num'rous Ills betray'd.
Oh had I rather un-admir'd remain'd
In some lone Isle, or distant *Northern* Land . . .
There kept my Charms conceal'd from mortal Eye,
Like Roses that in Desarts bloom and die—

(IV. 149–54, 157–8)

concludes with lines in which, an appealing victim, she presents
her other lock to the Baron as an object of further violation:

The Sister-Lock now sits uncouth, alone,
And in its Fellow's Fate foresees its own;
Uncurl'd it hangs, the fatal Sheers demands;
And tempts once more thy sacrilegious Hands.
Oh hadst thou, Cruel! been content to seize
Hairs less in sight, or any Hairs but these!

(IV. 171–6)

The sexual nuances in this passage are obvious, Earl R. Wasserman having rightly pointed out that the discerning contemporary
reader, familiar with classical literature, would have regarded the
lock as totemic, and the Baron as having raped the ritualistic sign
of Belinda's virginity.[5] And given the final reference to still more
unambiguous 'hairs'—a reference which arguably makes unequivocal Belinda's willingness to accept the Baron as a flesh and
blood, 'earthly lover'—one is invited to contemplate the terms on
which she would have allowed the totemic to become actual.

These may be inferred from the larger context in which this
reference occurs. In the first place one should note that there is a
significant difference between having the final couplet spoken by
Belinda, and hearing it from the lips of Thalestris (as in the two-
canto version). Thalestris is, after all, a far more conventional and
characteristic representative of the *beau monde*, for when she indig-
nantly laments the loss of the lock earlier in canto IV, she invokes
the empty and vulgarized concept of 'Honour', the social virtue of
mere appearances, of which the preservation had in the very first
canto been represented as the prerogative of the sylphs:

Gods! shall the Ravisher display your Hair,
While the Fops envy, and the Ladies stare!
Honour forbid! at whose unrival'd Shrine
Ease, Pleasure, Virtue, All, our Sex resign.
Methinks already I your Tears survey,
Already hear the horrid things they say,
Already see you a degraded Toast,
And all your Honour in a Whisper lost!
How shall I, then, your helpless Fame defend?
'Twill then be Infamy to seem your Friend!

(IV. 103–12)

Moreover, whereas in the earlier version the juxtaposition of speeches had created the impression of a young heroine more under the influence of her female companion, in the revised *Rape* Belinda appears as a heroine who has clearly come of age. This impression of an altogether more mature and commanding figure is conveyed by her obvious poise, her behaviour at the card-table, and a reaction very different from Thalestris's to Umbriel's attempt to touch her 'with Chagrin' (IV. 77).[6] But perhaps the clearest indication of this shift in emphasis can be found in the revisions that occur at the beginning of canto II. The four lines of the earlier version,

> *Belinda* rose, and 'midst attending Dames
> Launch'd on the Bosom of the silver *Thames*:
> A Train of well-drest Youths around her shone,
> And ev'ry Eye was fixed on her alone,

become in the later version:

> Not with more Glories, in th' Etherial Plain,
> The Sun first rises o'er the purpled Main,
> Than issuing forth, the Rival of his Beams
> Lanch'd on the Bosom of the Silver *Thames*.
> Fair Nymphs, and well-drest Youths around her shone,
> But ev'ry Eye was fix'd on her alone.

Here Belinda is surrounded, not by 'attending Dames' and ad-
miring youths, but by a mixed company of her own age-group
which nevertheless admires her as its radiantly beautiful centre.
Thus the lines that follow would seem to have a force denied them
in the earlier version. Whereas there the 'lively looks' of, so to
speak, a chaperoned heroine betray no preference for any member
of the opposite sex, in the later version she is apparently free to
show such a preference should she want to. That she does not,
and, without 'offending', bestows merely 'smiles' on all and
'favours' to none, may be explained by the fact that the 'earthly
lover' whom we later find 'lurking at her heart' is not of the group
—a reasonable inference given that the Baron has not so far been
introduced into the action of the poem.[7]

That Belinda, in alluding to 'any Hairs but these', is not merely
appealing to the Baron to salve her 'honour', but indeed hinting
at her own conscious and more sophisticated choice, is an impression reinforced by the classical parallel with which canto V opens.
When, implicitly compared with Dido, she makes her appeal to
Baron Aeneas, one may fittingly remember that Virgil's heroine
had regarded her first encounter with the Trojan as equivalent to
marriage (*coniugium vocat*).[8] Yet, though Belinda's appeal to the
Baron has the effect of making 'the pitying Audience melt in
Tears' (V. 1), he himself remains unmoved by her entreaties: 'But
Fate and *Jove* had stopp'd the *Baron*'s Ears' (V. 2). By representing
him as even more 'fixt' (V. 5) than the Trojan hero, Pope arguably
succeeds in granting him a certain stature beyond that of the conventional beau or philanderer. Of far more importance, however,
for our interpretation of this episode is the fact that the Aeneas-
Dido parallel would probably have ensured that the contemporary
reader, like the poem's own 'pitying Audience', was disposed to
sympathize with Belinda, and not in any way with the Baron.
Though the full significance of Lorenzo's words in *The Merchant
of Venice*—

> In such a night
> Stood Dido with a willow in her hand
> Upon the wild sea banks, and waft her love
> To come again to Carthage—
>
> (V. i. 9–12)

is perhaps open to some debate, they may—seeing that the 'willow' symbolized forsaken love (cf. *Faerie Queene*, I. i. 9, and the 'willow' song in *Othello*)—be taken to express some sympathy for this abandoned, faithful, lover. More clear-cut still is Chaucer's treatment of the Aeneas-Dido story in *The Hous of Fame* (of part of which Pope had produced a version before he wrote *The Rape of the Lock*). There Dido is presented as blameless and Aeneas as the faithless lover against whom the author's moral censure is wholly directed: 'For he to hir a traytour was' (I. 267). Thus Pope's Aeneas-Dido parallel arguably serves to place the Baron with respect to the central action. And even though it were to be assumed that Chaucer's retelling of this story should not influence our respective attitudes towards Belinda and the Baron, it would still have to be admitted that in Virgil, too, Dido is rejected by Aeneas, and not the other way round. Belinda, then, does not, as has been so widely and surprisingly assumed, reject the Baron. Instead it is the Baron who initially rejects Belinda.

Critics seem to have been influenced in taking the opposite view largely by their interpretation of Clarissa's speech as good moral advice that Belinda unaccountably fails to accept. But it should be clear that the heroine is now in a difficult position. She can hardly be expected to condone the 'rape' with a bland acquiescence; even Williams admits that her response to it is, from the viewpoint of hers or perhaps any society, 'perfectly natural'.[9] And it would have been impossible for her to have suggested directly to the Baron the best course of action for salving her honour. All she can do is hint at this by appearing before him as a victim prepared to suffer further at his hands. When, however, he shows no sympathy and ignores this appeal, she surely has no alternative but to protest in the only way now left her. It is, of course, true that for the contemporary reader of 1717—particularly the reader aware of the occasion which had prompted the first version of the poem—the tenor of Clarissa's speech, in advising the heroine to display 'good humour', might have slyly recalled the fact that the snipping of Arabella Fermor's lock had originally been greeted by an inordinate amount of fuss. Yet for all its obvious and undisputed good sense in the abstract, this speech has, in its immediate context, a curious irrelevance which sorts ill with the accepted view that Clarissa is Pope's mouthpiece. Far from 'scorning' a man, Belinda herself has just been rejected by the Baron. Nor can we conclude, notwithstanding her beauty and love of society, and also a certain measure of spirited (though understandable) daring in her approach to the game of love, that she has shown herself to be deficient in 'good sense' in making her appeal to the Baron. Thus Clarissa's words make no real contribution to the heroine's immediate plight. As the rejected woman, she plainly cannot endorse the wisdom they contain in any way that could materially alter the situation in which she finds herself.

It is therefore worth suggesting, especially since Clarissa had been the very character to give the Baron the scissors in the first place, that the following note on this speech, which is attributed to Pope in Warburton's edition, may not all be his:

> A new Character introduced in the subsequent Editions, to open more clearly the MORAL of the Poem, in a parody of the speech of Sarpedon to Glaucus in Homer.[10]

It is certain only that the last eleven words—'a parody of the speech of Sarpedon to Glaucus in Homer'—were written by Pope. To me the others sound suspiciously like Warburton's; and it is surely likely that he, rather than the author, would have referred to Clarissa as 'a new character'. As a parody of Sarpedon's speech, of which Pope had published his translation in 1709, Clarissa's is close and felicitous. According to Ralph Cohen, 'Sarpedon speaks with sublime rhetoric to encourage his friend and the warriors to battle. It is Clarissa's purpose in colloquial language to persuade Belinda to desist from battle.'[11] But may not Clarissa's speech also be regarded as providing an ironic contrast with its Homeric parallel in the further sense that Belinda is in no position to take Clarissa's advice? Certainly its occurrence immediately after she has been rejected by the Baron would seem to suggest as much. There is, moreover, a further hint that Pope might have intended subtly to undercut the role of 'grave Clarissa' who, with such prim archness, 'graceful wav'd her Fan' (V. 7). Both she and Pam

(the Jack of Clubs in the card-game) are connected, however
indirectly, through the figure of Sarpedon, since the line signal-
izing the defeat of Pam (the highest card in the game of Loo)—
'Falls undistinguish'd by the Victor *Spade*' (III. 64)—echoes the
following line from Pope's description of the death of Sarpedon:
'Lies undistinguish'd from the vulgar dead' (Pope's *Iliad*, XVI.
776). As William Frost has pointed out, Pope may have translated this passage by 1709[12]—though it was not published until
1718, the year after Clarissa's speech was added to *The Rape of the
Lock*. And so skilled was Pope at literary cross-echoes that it cannot be definitely stated that a connection between Clarissa and
Pam was unintentional. If it were intended, then we must conclude that, however worthy Clarissa or Pam might appear in a
different context, the role assigned to each of them in the action
of the poem is distinctly inconsequential.

If the above is a legitimate reading of events in the crucial fifth
canto, what are we to make of those other episodes in the poem
which seem to critics so unequivocally to suggest that Belinda is a
coquette? And how is one to interpret the significance of the
sylphic-gnomic 'machinery'? Moreover, to what extent is the
kind of love-interest already noted a motif that recurs throughout
the rest of the poem?

Though these are questions that perhaps cannot be definitively
answered, they invite consideration here for two main reasons. If
I have interpreted correctly the significance of the Aeneas-Dido
parallel, then the current view of Belinda would seem to make
Pope guilty of an inconsistency. Moreover, to maintain, as recent
critics have done, that only one interpretation of Belinda is
possible from the outset is to ignore what may be regarded as the
wit of Pope's portrayal of his heroine and, indeed, of the poem's
overall conception.

Because of the impression Belinda creates of a dazzling and un-
approachable beauty, it is inevitable that her eyes strike the 'gazers'

with full force (II. 13), and that many of her actions appear to
border on coquetry. Her locks, for example, were nourished 'to
the Destruction of Mankind' (II. 19ff.)—though Pope's use of this
phrase may, in its context, be expressive of consequence rather
than of purpose. And her approach to the card-table suggests an
element of *hubris* to which the 'rape' itself may seem a fitting
sequel:

> *Belinda* now, whom Thirst of Fame invites,
> Burns to encounter Two adventurous Knights,
> At *Ombre* singly to decide their Doom;
> And swells her Breast with Conquests yet to come.
>
> (III. 25–8)

Yet the accepted view of Belinda raises difficulties which none of
its proponents seems ready to admit. If she is to be regarded, in
Reichard's words, as 'a coquette *par excellence*',[13] how are we to
explain her willingness to entertain the idea of an 'earthly lover',
or the force of her later appeal to the Baron? And even if it were
to be answered that she changes from being a coquette at the
moment when the Baron approaches with the scissors, one would
still have to ask why it is that critics insist her later behaviour in
canto IV is indicative of coquettish prudery.

But perhaps a more serious objection to the accepted view of
Belinda is its failure to acknowledge the fascinating complexity
that Pope exploits in developing his theme. Much of the wit he
showed in acceding to Caryll's request, and especially in later en-
larging his poem to even more felicitous proportions, resides in
the ambiguity with which his heroine is presented—an ambiguity
that, in the five-canto version, is not merely more extensive but
only finally resolved when the reader experiences the kind of
surprise that inevitably accompanies the explicit reference to
Belinda's 'earthly lover'. This surprise is, of course, increased as
a result of the manner in which she approaches the card-table, for
the impression there created is, as we shall later see, only subtly
and implicitly modified by the presentation of the game itself. In

general, however, it may be said that Pope, even as he seems
to characterize Belinda most nearly as a coquette, continually
allows for the possibility of a different interpretation of her
character.

While it is obviously true that the whole poem, despite its
originally favourable reception by the real-life counterpart of the
heroine, ostensibly reflects a playfully condescending attitude
towards women, the present tendency to regard Belinda in a
morally unfavourable light seems to me not only to make nonsense of the poem's occasional nature, but also to ignore the
genuine ambiguities that, at least prior to the 'rape', are inherent
in the text. There is, admittedly, more opportunity for such
ambiguity (or, as recent critics would argue, moral censure of
the heroine) in the five-canto version, which introduces both the
dressing-table scene and the sylphic-gnomic machinery. Yet the
comparison of Belinda with the sun, which has been taken as one
of the episodes most damaging to her character, is also present in
the two-canto version. And the following line is, in fact, common
to all three versions: 'This ev'n *Belinda* may vouchsafe to view' (I.
4). This line may be regarded as highlighting the whole problem
of Pope's ambiguity of presentation. 'Vouchsafe' could mean
'deign' or 'condescend', with sly overtones that it is in Belinda's
interest to heed what is said of her. But it seems *prima facie* more
likely that the line should be taken to imply that what is said of
her is meant to be complimentary. At any rate it may be assumed
that it gave Miss Fermor no offence when she first read the two-
canto version of the poem in manuscript.

It would seem to be Pope's intention in the 'epic proposition'—
'What dire Offence from am'rous Causes springs' (1. 1.)—to suggest the presence of a love motif that recurs throughout the poem.
And arguably this motif makes its appearance in the five-canto
version early in canto I. After describing Shock's action in waking
the heroine, Pope continues:

'Twas then *Belinda!* if Report say true,
Thy Eyes first open'd on a *Billet-doux.*

(I. 116–17)

On this the Twickenham editor, referring the reader to the famous
'Puffs, Powders, Patches, Bibles, Billet-doux' (I. 138), trenchantly
comments: 'Report was a liar.' Read in this way, the lines provide
a good example of Pope's ironic attitude towards Belinda. Yet it
is possible, perhaps, also to read them as an example of his tactful
decorum: loath to intrude at this point, the poet confines himself
to reporting that Belinda saw a love-letter when she first opened
her eyes. Certainly this interpretation fits in better with the action
that subsequently develops between herself and the Baron. If it
can be assumed that the letter is from him, it will—at least in retro-
spect—cause no surprise that it is capable of dispelling all thoughts
of Ariel's appearance to her in a dream. Nor does the apparently
ironic reference to '*Wounds, Charms,* and *Ardors*' (I. 119) make this
interpretation less likely since on one level it continues the playful
realism of 'And sleepless Lovers, just at Twelve, awake' (I. 16).
One may even suggest that the exaggerated style of this letter's
protestations is peculiarly apt given that the Baron is later to show
himself as apparently no more sincere than the conventional beau.

But the scene in canto I that has been thought to cast most
doubt on Belinda's moral reputation is the famous description of
her toilette. According to Reichard, 'she displays herself most
vividly in what is perhaps the purplest of the poem's purple
passages—the ritual at her dressing-table', where, like Narcissus
or Milton's Eve, she practises 'not beauty-worship, but self-
worship'.[14] J. S. Cunningham, too, though more aware of the
danger of 'turning a satirical comedy of manners into a too severe
and single-minded *exemplum* on the errors of her ways', regards
this episode as a 'ritual of self-adoration . . . enacted in a moral
vacuum'.[15] And Cleanth Brooks's view that 'she puts on her divinity at her dressing table'[16] is also expressed by Cohen, who sees
this 'painting oneself into godhood' as an example of the kind of
'transformation' that is indicative of a serious inversion of values.[17]

It is now accepted that Warburton was wrong to find in this

description of Belinda's toilette 'a small inaccuracy'; as the Twickenham editor has pointed out, Belinda is represented as both 'goddess' and 'chief priestess'. Yet it may, even so, be too limiting to suggest that the reference to 'the sacred Rites of Pride' (I. 128) is to be unambiguously interpreted as Pope's satire on an act of out-and-out self-adoration. 'A heav'nly Image in the Glass appears' (I. 125) before the effects achieved by 'the *Cosmetic Pow'rs*' are described; and it would seem to be these 'powers' that

> the Nymph intent adores
> With Head uncover'd.
>
> (I. 123–4)

That the lady of fashion had at her disposal 'the various Off'rings of the World' (I. 130) could be regarded as evidence of a providentially ordered universe;[18] and such a view certainly harmonizes with the mythopoeic stature granted to Belinda, who in this episode is appropriately 'deck'd with all that Land and Sea afford' (V. 11). Even Clarissa has no unfavourable comment to make on the beauty who shows herself to be 'the first in Virtue, as in Face' (V. 18); indeed, though it had been common to associate face-painting with moral laxity, and especially with adultery or pride, there was a body of contemporary opinion which defended it as entirely 'lawful'. For example, the author (supposedly 'a learned Bishop', perhaps Jeremy Taylor) of *Several Letters between Two Ladies, wherein the Lawfulness and Unlawfulness of Artificial Beauty in Point of Conscience are nicely debated* (1701), in setting out to obviate 'the Objections of those Precise [i.e. Puritanical] ones, who rail at this innocent support of Nature's outward Form', not only cited Ezekiel XVI as an example of the proper use that might be made of 'the fruit of Divine Munificence', but recognized that the whole question could not be discussed in the abstract without reference to 'the End or Mind of those that doe it'. This willingness to admit the importance of motive is obviously relevant to Pope's presentation of Belinda; and with it may also be linked the 'learned Bishop's' view that painting the face is merely one of the 'venial Vanities of humane Life', and 'so far sin or not sin in the conscience of the Doer, as their Minds are morally and intentionally disposed'.[19]

Though, in his later *Epistle to a Lady*, Pope was to emphasize the incongruity of 'Sappho at her toilet's greasy task' and 'Sappho fragrant at an ev'ning Mask' in terms that engender loathing and disgust (ll. 25ff.), his tone in the *Rape* is, of course, entirely different. Belinda's toilette only succeeds in making her 'heav'nly Image' appear even more beautiful: making-up 'calls forth' all the inherent 'Wonders of her Face'. Ultimately the question one must try to answer in attempting to evaluate her moral character is what were her hidden motives for engaging in this elaborate ceremony or ritual. Admittedly the dressing-table scene, parodying as it does the arming of the epic hero (cf. I. 139), may on one level be read as indicative of her willingness to encounter 'adventurous Knights' from among the opposite sex. Yet since beauty, as Clarissa herself implies (cf. V. 15–16), obviously plays a necessary part in sending home the shaft of love to men's hearts, the question whether Belinda makes up because she is a thorough-going coquette, or because she primarily wishes to make a conquest of the heart of a particular 'earthly lover', can only be resolved in the light of the poem's ensuing action. Though her approach to the card-table arguably displays an element of *hubris*, the way in which the game itself is played out suggests, as we shall later see, her willingness to triumph over but a single opponent in this formalized enactment of the love-duel. Moreover, even though late in canto V she assumes a virago-like role that is a credible extension of the earlier image, it should be remembered that she has by this time already been rejected by the Baron, and that any other course of action on her part would have seemed both unnatural and entirely devoid of spirit.

Pope's reference to 'the sacred Rites of Pride' in the dressing-table scene is further complicated by the following couplet of canto II:

> Yet graceful Ease, and Sweetness void of Pride,
> Might hide her Faults, if *Belles* had Faults to hide.

(II. 15–16)

The straightforward reading of this couplet in the two-canto version of the poem is that Belinda possesses 'graceful Ease, and Sweetness void of Pride'. In the five-canto version it could just conceivably be taken to mean that if Belinda were to show 'graceful Ease, and Sweetness void of Pride' then her faults would be hidden by these qualities. But she is clearly possessed of 'graceful Ease'; and if her 'faults' do not include 'pride', the necessity for such a tortuous reading becomes pointless. To put the matter another way, if 'pride' is one of the 'faults' that need to be hidden, then Belinda presumably needs to cultivate also the 'graceful Ease' that she already possesses. It is hard to make anything but nonsense of the lines unless we assume that the 'pride' to which they refer is not to be numbered among her 'faults'.

The possibility therefore remains that the earlier phrase, 'the sacred Rites of Pride'—where the 'pride' seems specifically associated with the 'rites' or ritual of the toilette—is Pope's suitably exaggerated way of referring to female vanity in a poem which, as I have said, ostensibly reflects a playfully condescending attitude towards women. In dedicating to Miss Fermor the five-canto version, the poet states that 'it was intended only to divert a few young Ladies, who have good Sense and good Humour enough, to laugh not only at their Sex's little unguarded Follies, but at their own'. More explicit is his notably moralistic letter to Mrs (or Miss) Marriot, in which Pope implies that the 'satire' of his poem —'the most inoffensive, of anything of mine' and 'a sort of writing very like tickling'—is directed against 'the vain ones of your own sex'.[20] There is, moreover, some evidence to suggest that an important distinction might legitimately be made between 'vanity' and 'pride'. In his *Thoughts on Various Subjects* Swift was to point out, not only that 'the Self-Love of some Men inclines them to please others; and the Self-Love of others is wholly employed in pleasing themselves', but also that 'to be vain is rather a mark of Humility than Pride'. He was accordingly led to conclude: 'I therefore deliver it as a Maxim; that whoever desires the Character of a proud Man, ought to conceal his Vanity'.[21]

Though Swift was also to observe that 'Love of Flattery in most Men proceeds from the mean Opinion they have of themselves:

In Women from the contrary',[22] Belinda's vanity is, given the poem's love motif, not so much damning as understandable. What critics have assumed to be an act of 'self-adoration' or 'self-worship', and as therefore thoroughly characteristic of the co-quette, can be regarded, in effect at least, as her way of ensuring at her own 'altar' to Love, her dressing-table, that she will be pleasing to others. Or perhaps we should say 'one other' seeing that this episode follows on her receipt of the love-letter, and that Ariel is to be finally routed by 'an earthly lover lurking at her heart'.

The dressing-table scene can therefore be interpreted in the light of an incipient love-interest that has already been hinted at. And it is, I suggest, within the same framework or context that one should interpret the description of Belinda at the beginning of canto II. This has usually been taken to exemplify sheer coquetry; Reichard, for example, stating that 'there is no ambiguity in the girl's performance on the Thames Barge', describes this as 'a tour de force of flirtation'.[23] The explicit comparison of Belinda with the sun is what makes this episode so unambiguous for most critics. Cohen concludes: 'It is apparent that what is natural for the sun is unnatural for Belinda'.[24] And the editors of the recent volume devoted to the poem in the Literary Casebook Series are merely voicing accepted opinion when they note that the line 'And, like the Sun, they shine on all alike' (II. 14) 'develops the simile complimenting Belinda's radiant eyes, but becomes ironic, satirically suggesting that she is an indiscriminate coquette and even, perhaps, a slightly stupid coquette'.[25] Yet not only is the tone of the earlier conceit—

> *Sol* thro' white Curtains shot a tim'rous Ray,
> And op'd those Eyes that must eclipse the Day—
>
> (I. 13–14)

undeniably complimentary, but the later comparison with the sun further extends the felt significance of the heroine's role. The effect of this comparison, which suggests that the central action is of almost cosmic proportions, is further subtly confirmed both by the Rosicrucian machinery, and by the subsequent description of the card-game.

That Belinda's world is shot through with the exquisitely shimmering beauty of the sylphs is universally acknowledged and needs no demonstration. Consistently with the comparison at the beginning of canto II, 'the fields of purest Æther' (II. 77) become an inevitable part of the poem's range of associations. Yet there seems to me enough ambiguity surrounding the part played by the Rosicrucian machinery in the action of the poem to give some substance to the view of Pope's contemporary John Dennis which Johnson reports as follows in his *Life of Pope*:

> It is remarked by Dennis likewise that the machinery is superfluous; that by all the bustle of preternatural operation the main event is neither hastened nor retarded. To this charge an efficacious answer is not easily made.[26]

It is at least possible, as Ian Jack suggests, that Pope's Rosicrucian machinery is meant to parody that use of 'Guardian Angels' in heroic verse which had been recommended by Dryden and practised by Cowley.[27] And if such were Pope's intention, it is I believe, legitimate to reconsider the larger function of this machinery, and in particular whether, though in some sense providing a subtle accompaniment to the central action, it is ever able completely to subsume the heroine into its beautiful and grotesque worlds.

Though a comparison has sometimes been made between Belinda and Milton's Eve,[28] the closest parallel with *Paradise Lost* is when Ariel appears to Pope's heroine in a dream:[29]

> . . . (That ev'n in Slumber caus'd her Cheek to glow)
> Seem'd to her Ear his winning Lips to lay,
> And thus in Whispers said, or seem'd to say.

(I. 24–6)

And certainly for a 'Guardian *Sylph*' (I. 20) Ariel seems to be at

some pains to convince Belinda that he fulfils this role: 'If e'er . . .'
(I. 29); 'Hear and believe! . . .' (I. 35); 'Know then . . .' (I. 41);
'Know farther yet . . .' (I. 67); 'Of these am I, who thy Protection
claim' (I. 105, my italics). Even though the influence of the sylphs
on Belinda's appearance is more directly acknowledged in the
concluding lines of the dressing-table scene, one is left with the
impression that, in the earlier scene, Belinda has probably been
the victim of that 'mimic fancy' which, as Adam explains to Eve,
operates 'most in dreams' (*Paradise Lost*, V. 110ff.). It is therefore probably not too much of an exaggeration to suggest that
the scene in which Ariel's dream is dispelled by the contents of
Belinda's love-letter serves as an apt paradigm of this machinery's
whole metaphoric mode. At least it is clear that when, after the
card-game, the scene contracts to coffee in the drawing-room, the
contrast between the heroine and what the sylphs would have her
is nicely underlined:

> Sudden he [i.e. Ariel] view'd, in spite of all her Art,
> An Earthly Lover lurking at her Heart.
> Amaz'd, confus'd, he found his Pow'r expir'd,
> Resign'd to Fate, and with a Sigh retir'd.
>
> (III. 143–6)

Despite a beauty that would make her a universal toast, Belinda is
no longer, if she ever was, in the sylphs' power; her heart is no
longer, if it ever was, a 'moving Toyshop' (cf. I. 100). The pervasive zeugma—so wittily reflecting Ariel's view of 'Things
below' (I. 36) and, indeed, the operations of the world at large—
cannot, then, be finally interpreted as an implied censure on the
heroine. Losing her 'heart' at a ball is not of the same order as
losing her 'necklace' (II. 109)—though, of course, the sylphs will
resolutely mount an equal guard on each. Even as they incom-
parably enhance the beauty of the *beau monde*, and thus help to give
Belinda the stature of a nonpareil, they demonstrate their own
superficiality. That Ariel is powerless when confronted with a
challenge to the heroine's heart should alert the reader to the inherent absurdity of these sylphic cohorts in claiming so much

significance for themselves. Apart from Belinda's incidental reference to her earlier dream late in the fourth canto (when she has good reason to be somewhat suspicious of man, and when, significantly, she implies her former disbelief in what was revealed to her (IV. 165–6)), the sylphs reappear only once more, at the moment when her lock is stellified:

> The *Sylphs* behold it kindling as it flies,
> And pleas'd pursue its Progress thro' the Skies.
>
> (V. 131–2)

Nothing could better illustrate their charming but inconsequential passivity, or what may, I think, be described as the subservience of their role to Belinda's.

But what of the gnomic machinery which, since critics regard Belinda as 'too conscious' of her face (cf. I. 79), has been interpreted as appropriately touching her 'with Chagrin' (IV. 77)? Williams, as we have seen, attributes the origin of the ill-nature and affectation that supposedly makes her reject the Baron to 'the course of prudery delineated earlier in the Cave of Spleen episode'; while Cohen argues that 'since she does not acknowledge the earthly lover, she becomes the prey of Umbriel'.[30] Yet it is hard to conceive in what sense Belinda could have 'acknowledged' her earthly lover before the officious Umbriel made his journey to the Cave of Spleen. Nor in this fourth canto—and thus prior to her appeal to the Baron—does it seem to me that Belinda either is touched 'with Chagrin', or suffers from the inability traditionally ascribed to the splenetic person to see clearly or act rationally. When the gnome bursts his 'bag' over the heads of the heroine and Thalestris, Belinda, it is said, 'burns with more than mortal Ire' (IV. 93); but Thalestris, it would seem, has absorbed more than her share of this 'Force of Female Lungs' (IV. 83) since she makes a long, impassioned speech expressing her vulgarized conception of 'Honour', and then exhorts her beau, Sir Plume, to demand back (ineffectually, as it turns out) the severed lock. Umbriel, however, only rouses Belinda to complaint by subsequently breaking 'the Vial whence the Sorrows flow' (IV. 142). And then

she only shows 'chagrin' in the sense in which the *OED*, citing
the example from this canto, defines the word: 'that which frets or
worries the mind; . . . anxiety; melancholy'. In the sense of 'acute
vexation' (which the *OED* first attributes to Pope a couple of years
after the revised *Rape* appeared), Belinda does not show chagrin
until, in canto V, she has herself been rejected by the Baron. Only
then does Umbriel have his triumph, while his fellow-gnomes are
said to direct the grains of snuff with which the heroine begins to
get the better of her adversary. In canto IV, however, Belinda is
presented as a beautiful and pathetic figure for whom the audience's sympathy can be fittingly engaged:

> Then see! the *Nymph* in beauteous Grief appears,
> Her Eyes half-languishing, half-drown'd in Tears;
> On her heav'd Bosom hung her drooping Head,
> Which, with a Sigh, she rais'd; and thus she said.
>
> (IV. 143–6)

Surely no one can fail to notice that her appearance here is very
different from that of the frustrated and grotesque forms that inhabit Spleen's underworld. Once again the machinery has provided a background *against* which—rather than a context *within*
which—to interpret Belinda's actions.

Arguably the sylphic machinery, however decorative, has no
effective influence on the card-game—and this notwithstanding
that, as soon as Belinda 'spreads her Hand',

> th' Aerial Guard
> Descend, and sit on each important Card.
>
> (III. 31–2)

From this point onwards, the card-game takes over from the
sylphs the function of providing the central action with its larger
associations and significance. The heroic imagery, so felicitously
adapted to the court cards, and continued through every detail of
the 'Combat on the Velvet Plain' (III. 44), is extended by references first to trumps (the Queen of Spades becomes a 'warlike
Amazon', III. 67) and to colour, and then to the final 'trick', so

that the whole world—its peoples, battles and statecraft—is brought vividly before us.

Preparative of this is, of course, the zeugmatic opening of canto III, together with its gesture towards comprehensiveness:

> One speaks the Glory of the *British Queen*,
> And one describes a charming *Indian Screen*.
>
> (III. 13–14)

And this suggestion that the central action occurs within a wider context is continued in the lines that follow:

> The hungry Judges soon the Sentence sign,
> And wretches hang that Jury-men may Dine;
> The Merchant from th' *Exchange* returns in Peace,
> And the long Labours of the *Toilette* cease.
>
> (III. 21–4)

These lines have been interpreted as providing the most pointed satire of Belinda and her world.[31] Yet, in the light of the subsequent description of the card-game, the more ominous note sounded in the earlier couplet,

> Here *Britain*'s Statesmen oft the Fall foredoom
> Of Foreign Tyrants, and of Nymphs at home,
>
> (III. 5–6)

and especially in the juxtapositions of these later lines, can be regarded as having the effect of making the central action appear of greater (rather than lesser) moment. Certainly the action of the card-game is concretely realized in terms that suggest its momentous and universal significance:

> Thus when dispers'd a routed Army runs,
> Of *Asia*'s Troops, and *Africk*'s Sable Sons,
> With like Confusion different Nations fly,
> Of various Habit and of various Dye.
>
> (III. 81–4)

And since the moves and manoeuvres of this game provide a witty and formalized framework for the developing love-action, Belinda may be regarded as playing a game of life (not just of cards) of which the outcome is for her momentous.

This elaborately contrived centre-piece, which brings together many of the poem's subtle complications and motifs, is, in an important sense, the logical outcome of those earlier ceremonies represented by Belinda's toilette and the Baron's sacrificial altar to 'Love'. Notwithstanding the narrowly-avoided defeat of the heroine, one is left with the impression of both her human skill in this war-game between the sexes, and her Creator-like role in echoing Genesis at the card-table:

> The skilful Nymph reviews her Force with Care;
> *Let Spades be Trumps!* she said, and Trumps they were.
>
> (III. 45–6)

Thus the earlier suggestion of an element of *hubris* in her approach to the card-table is inevitably qualified by a sense of her implied influence on the turn of the game. The cards fall in a way that robs the third player of any significance;[32] and since this has the appearance of having been divinely willed as a result of Belinda's calling trumps, it would seem that she has herself been partly responsible for the fact that the Baron is her only opponent in the central love-duel.

It would seem, however, that the Baron is an unworthy opponent. When he first appears, he is described as 'adventurous' (II. 29); and in offering up a sacrifice to Love, he implores 'propitious Heav'n' (II. 36) to aid his quest. Yet there is, even so, a marked disingenuousness about the means he proposes to pursue:

> Resolv'd to win, he meditates the way,
> By Force to ravish, or by Fraud betray.
>
> (II. 31–2)

71

The reader's reaction is, nevertheless, immediately complicated by Pope's disarming juxtaposition, for the next couplet—

> For when Success a Lover's Toil attends,
> Few ask, if Fraud or Force attain'd his Ends—

can, despite the sly innuendo, be taken in its larger context to suggest that the Baron is himself a lover. 'Toil' is, of course, ambiguous, especially in view of the hunting, 'ensnaring' imagery of the preceding lines; yet the inference contained in II. 23-4,

> Love in these Labyrinths his Slaves detains,
> And mighty Hearts are held in slender Chains,

suggests that the Baron is indeed a 'slave' to Love, his 'mighty heart' being held captive by Belinda's tresses. The 'prize' to which he aspires (II. 30, 44) can apparently be interpreted to mean either the 'lock' (which would make him merely cold and calculating), or, by an expected synecdoche, Belinda herself. There is also an ostensible ambiguity in the description of the Baron's sacrificial fire. While he offers up such effects as may be compared with those of the deceased beau described in *Tatler* 113, he builds like Chaucer's Palamon, whose motives were of the purest, his altar to Love.

When Pope first wrote *The Rape of the Lock*, the portrayal of the Baron probably presented him with something of a problem; and since this part of the poem underwent no major revision, we may conclude that even in the five-canto version it reflects whatever was the poet's original intention. Pope had been asked to make a jest of an incident that had caused an estrangement between two prominent Catholic families; and if the Twickenham editor is right to suggest that this probably occurred during a 'period of circumspection' when Arabella Fermor was being considered as 'the possible bride for Lord Petre',[33] the poet would have needed to display a good deal of tact in the presentation of his two main characters. Though he might have suspected that the snipping of Arabella's lock would not lead to a marriage, he presumably could not be certain, or represent as certain in a negative sense, what Lord Petre's ultimate intentions might be. He could not therefore represent the Baron as merely a conventional beau or philanderer; and perhaps this is why he exploits the inherent ambiguity of his mock-heroic mode to give a certain ambivalence even to those scenes in which the Baron appears as most disingenuous. Certainly the ambiguity already noted is to some degree sustained throughout the entire poem. The passage in which the Baron is introduced after the card-game contains a seemingly unequivocal reference to mere scheming: he is inspired to 'New Stratagems, the radiant Lock to gain' (III. 120) in the manner of a 'politician' (or at least of the amateur politician who habitually frequented coffee-houses). But then comes the apostrophe, 'Ah cease rash Youth! desist ere 'tis too late', reminiscent of Homer's to Patroclus or Virgil's to Camilla, both warriors fated to die; and this is followed by an allusion to Scylla, whose love it was that prompted her to an act of treachery which held dire consequences for herself. The ambiguity is, indeed, sustained right up to the very moment of the 'rape' in that the Baron, in taking from Clarissa the instrument of mischief, does so 'with rev'rence' (III. 131).

In refusing to hand back Belinda's severed lock, the Baron makes it plain that he intends to wear in his ring, as a trophy for all the world to see, 'The long-contended Honours of her Head' (IV. 140). He also rejects Belinda, as Aeneas had rejected Dido. In the mêlée, however, that follows Clarissa's speech, when undisguised human nature breaks through the poem's decorously patterned surface of social conventions, he is described as one 'Who sought no more than on his Foe to die' (V. 78)—where 'die', as Geoffrey Tillotson has explained, 'bears the contemporary sense of reach (and pass) the point of sexual consummation'.[34] And when the victorious Belinda threatens him with a 'deadly *Bodkin*' (V. 88), his attitude becomes even more ambiguous still:

> Nor think, to die dejects my lofty Mind;
> All that I dread, is leaving you behind!
> Rather than so, ah let me still survive,
> And burn in *Cupid*'s Flames,—but burn alive.
>
> (V. 99–102)

In what sense, then, is the Baron a lover? This is a question to which Belinda's next words give special point, for they recall as Wasserman has pointed out, the cry of Ovid's 'young girls [*spoliatae puellae*] who fancy they are being earnestly wooed, only to find that their elegant suitors are inflamed only by a desire to steal their robes'.[35] Moreover, Pope wittily sustains both the surface ambivalence and his own seemingly more unambiguous interpretation of the Baron's actions by placing 'Lovers' Hearts' (V. 118) among the lost, absurd or discredited things to be found in 'the Lunar Sphere' (V. 113). If the Baron is indeed a lover, his heart certainly merits no less equivocal an abode! But Belinda's lock passes beyond this changeable and fickle region, fittingly taking its place, like the lock of the faithful Berenice, among the stars.

Both the stellification of Belinda's lock and the earlier Aeneas-Dido parallel had been features of the two-canto version of the poem, and to its original readers skilled in detecting literary cross-echoes, Baron-Aeneas might even have seemed to be implicated in this final stellification. When Aeneas meets Dido in the underworld, he addresses her with the words:[36]

> per sidera iuro,
> per superos, et si qua fides tellure sub ima est,
> invitus, regina, tuo de litore cessi.

And in Catullus's poem on Berenice, the severed and stellified lock swears in words that echo Virgil's:[37]

> invita, o regina, tuo de vertice cessi,
> invita: adiuro teque tuumque caput,
> digna ferat quod siquis inaniter adiurarit.

Even though it cannot be assumed from the text of the *Rape* that the Baron feels, or is meant to feel, if only by implication, any of Aeneas's regret for the way that things have turned out, it seems plausible to suggest that the significance of the allusions—one might almost say the *hidden* allusions—in the final canto of the poem would not have been lost on those most involved in the real-life situation that provided its immediate occasion. While the poem is in some sense appropriately open-ended, with the stellification of Belinda's lock being a decorous way of resolving, or rather suspending, the central action, the overall impression is that any further initiative capable of providing a happier outcome for one or both of the parties concerned must come from the Baron himself. Though Lord Petre did not give any earnest of assurance to Miss Fermor or her family, Pope, when he wrote the poem, had nevertheless to assume that such an assurance might still be given. Thus the Baron-Aeneas parallel must have seemed especially felicitous in that it could be interpreted as calculated to remind Lord Petre of an implied obligation to the lady. Arguably it even left the way open for him to feel a sense of regret should he want to.

Nor could Pope allow subsequent events to place Arabella in a ridiculous light, and it is, I suggest, for this reason that the love motif is presented throughout the *Rape* with such delicate obliquity. Certainly the two-canto version, which does not include the reception of the love-letter, the dressing-table scene, the Rosicrucian machinery, the card-game, or the explicit reference to Belinda's 'earthly lover', has the effect of making the love-interest even more implicit at the same time as it suggests more obviously the pathos of the young heroine's position. And that Arabella was so willing to show the manuscript of it about to her friends suggests that Pope had, in every respect, struck just the right note. But the poet could not guard against every possible contingency; and since Arabella's attitude towards the poem changed so markedly after it was published, the Twickenham editor may be right to suggest that this was due to the fact that Lord Petre had meantime married a younger and much richer lady.[38]

Doubtless Lord Petre's marriage prompted the kind of gossip unfavourable to Arabella that would of itself have soured her reaction to the poem. And if a number of contemporary readers viewed Belinda in the same light as do most modern critics, this gossip could only have become particularly pointed. By the time he came to publish his enlarged version, Pope felt that something was needed to restore the lady's reputation, and a letter to Caryll outlines the careful measures he took to try to prevent any further scandal:[39]

> As to the Rape of the *Lock*, I believe I have managed the dedication so nicely that it can neither hurt the lady, nor the author. I writ it very lately, and upon great deliberation; the young lady approves of it; and the best advice in the kingdom, of the men of sense has been made use of in it, even to the Treasurer's. A preface which salved the lady's honour, without affixing her name, was also prepared, but by herself superseded in favour of the dedication. Not but that, after all, fools will talk, and fools will hear 'em.

In his dedication Pope stresses that 'the Human Persons are as Fictitious as the Airy ones; and the Character of *Belinda*, as it is now manag'd, resembles You in nothing but in Beauty'. Yet Miss Fermor would have realized that such a dedication could only further the association of herself with Belinda. Perhaps it was vanity that prompted her to choose to be openly linked with Pope's beautiful heroine. She may even have relished the thought of being identified with one who could encounter with such apparent willingness and success 'two adventurous Knights'. Certainly the tone of the letter Pope was to write to her on her subsequent marriage suggests that there might have been something in her recent conduct to justify its veiled admonition.[40] At any rate, it is on record that when Johnson and Mrs Thrale, many years later, visited her niece in Paris, the latter remembered that 'Mr Pope's praise made her aunt very troublesome and conceited'.[41]

Yet whatever the truth of this, we cannot assume that Belinda herself is the victim of self-centred pride. However coquettish the real-life Arabella might have become, the heroine of the revised *Rape* arguably shows herself as beautiful, assured, possessed of a proper measure of daring in her approach to the game of love, and ultimately willing to accept on honourable terms an 'earthly lover'. In her character as well as in her person, she may, then, be regarded as superior to that world which nevertheless derives such brilliance from her presence. And if Arabella Fermor was, not surprisingly, unequal to the task of carrying off the part of Pope's heroine in real life, she must have been confined by her own more obvious limitations, and those of a world that did not enjoy the untrammelled freedom of great art.

Notes

1 'The Love Affair in Pope's *Rape of the Lock*', in *Alexander Pope: The Rape of the Lock*, ed. David G. Lougee and Robert W. McHenry, Jr (The Merrill Literary Casebook Series: Columbus, Ohio, 1969), pp. 83–4.

2 Earl R. Wasserman, 'The Limits of Allusion in *The Rape of the Lock*', in *Twentieth Century Interpretations of The Rape of the Lock*, ed. G. S. Rousseau (Englewood Cliffs, N.J., 1969), p. 82.

3 *The Rape of the Lock and Other Poems* (London, 1962, 3rd ed.), p. 90. Tillotson, in support of this view, quotes the following couplet from I. 9–10:

> Oh say what stranger Cause, yet unexplor'd,
> Cou'd make a gentle *Belle* reject a *Lord*?

And in his note he glosses 'unexplor'd' as 'undiscovered' in the now obsolete sense of the word found in Pope's *Messiah*, 49ff.: '. . . the good shepherd . . . Explores the lost, the wand'ring sheep directs'. According to this gloss Pope's couplet must mean: 'What hitherto unknown or undiscovered cause . . .'. But the meaning of 'unexplor'd' may be closer to the sense of the word found in Pope's translation of the first book of the *Iliad* (published 1715)—

> But let some Prophet, or some sacred Sage,
> Explore the Cause of great *Apollo*'s Rage (83–4)

where the meaning is 'seek to ascertain or find out'. Thus 'yet unexplor'd' could mean that the poet—given that the 'Muse' is here exhorted to 'say'—has still to seek to ascertain or find out the reason for such extraordinary behaviour. The 'stranger Cause' of Belinda's behaviour can, then, only be discovered from the poem itself.

4 'The "Fall" of China and *The Rape of the Lock*', in *Pope: The Rape of the Lock*, ed. Lougee and McHenry, p. 127.

5 'The Limits of Allusion in *The Rape of the Lock*', in *Twentieth Century Interpretations*, pp. 72–3.

6 Cf. *ante*, pp. 68–9. One may also note the subtle change from 'Sorrow's Pomp' (1712: II. 59) to 'beauteous Grief' in the later version (IV. 143).

7 It seems to me indisputable, both from the lines immediately prior to the 'rape' (cf. III. 131ff.), and from the way in which the cardgame is presented (cf. *ante*, p. 71), that the Baron is to be identified as the 'earthly lover'.

8 *Aeneid*, IV. 172. It is interesting to note that Pope's phrase 'anxious Cares' (IV. 1), which is applied to Belinda, echoes Dryden's translation of the 'anxious Cares' that Dido felt on beholding Aeneas.

9 'The "Fall" of China and *The Rape of the Lock*', in *Pope: The Rape of the Lock*, p. 124.

10 Cf. *The Rape of the Lock and Other Poems*, pp. 197 n., 395. Though Pope, in annotating many years later his copy of *Remarks on Mr. Pope's Rape of the Lock* (1728), countered Dennis's charge that the poem lacked an obvious moral by writing in the margin 'Clarissas Speach', this cannot be taken as irrefutable evidence of his intention as expressed in the poem. In *An Epistle to Dr. Arbuthnot* (ll. 147ff.), he was, moreover, to include *The Rape of the Lock* among those earlier verses in which 'pure Description held the place of Sense'.

11 'Transformation in *The Rape of the Lock*', *Eighteenth-Century Studies*, II (1968–9), 216.

12 '*The Rape of the Lock* and Pope's Homer', *Modern Language Review*, VIII (1947), 347.

13 'The Love Affair in Pope's *Rape of the Lock*', in *Pope: The Rape of the Lock*, p. 85.

14 *Ibid.*, pp. 90, 92.

15 *Pope: The Rape of the Lock* (London, 1961), pp. 39, 41, 47.

16 'The Case of Miss Arabella Fermor', in *Twentieth Century Interpretations*, p. 23.

17 'Transformation in *The Rape of the Lock*', p. 209.

18 See Louis A. Landa, 'Of Silkworms and Farthingales and the Will of God: An Aspect of Eighteenth-Century Rationalism', a paper read to the Second David Nichol Smith Memorial Seminar, and to be published in the forthcoming volume of proceedings. Cf. *Windsor Forest*, ll. 392ff., for Pope's view of the benefits of worldwide commerce.

19 Sigg. A3–A3ᵛ, pp. 28, 148, 154, 159. Cf. *Athenian Oracle*, II (London, 1703), 33.

20 *The Correspondence of Alexander Pope*, ed. George Sherburn (Oxford,

1956), I. 211. Pope adds: 'I am so vain as to fancy a pretty complete picture of the life of our modern ladies in this idle town from which you are so happily, so prudently, and so philosophically retired'. Even if he had never written, later the same year, his *To a Young Lady, on her leaving the Town after the Coronation*, it would be wrong to interpret his remarks in this letter too sombrely. His observation that its recipient should not be made to pass 'one quarter of an hour of all [her] life ill in reading such impertinence' as his letter is an expression of that conventionally pious sentiment, so common-place in the century, which occurs in his very next letter to Sir William Trumbull.

21 *A Proposal for Correcting the English Tongue, Polite Conversation, Etc.,* ed. Herbert Davis, with Louis Landa (Oxford, 1957), pp. 243, 245.

22 *Ibid.,* p. 246.

23 'The Love Affair in Pope's *Rape of the Lock*', in *Pope: The Rape of the Lock,* p. 87.

24 'Transformation in *The Rape of the Lock*', p. 208.

25 *Pope: The Rape of the Lock,* p. 8.

26 *Lives of the Poets,* ed. Hill, III. 235.

27 *Augustan Satire: Intention and Idiom in English Poetry 1660–1750* (Oxford, 1965 reprint), p. 81.

28 Cf. *ante,* p. 61.

29 Cf. *Paradise Lost,* IV. 800ff.; V. 10, 35ff.

30 'Transformation in *The Rape of the Lock*', p. 222.

31 Wasserman, for example, citing Homeric sources for these lines, states that Pope transforms Homer's judges by making 'something hideous and savage of their eighteenth-century heirs, who sacrifice lives under selfish compulsion of their own bodily hunger' ('The Limits of Allusion in *The Rape of the Lock*', in *Twentieth Century Interpretations,* p. 71). But the reference to 'hungry Judges' was a common jibe. Moreover, in Pope's lines, the judges merely 'sign' the sentence 'that jurymen may dine'—a practice which in itself need not imply a summary execution of justice since, according to a later statute of George II, it was laid down as necessary judicial procedure that death sentences had to be pronounced immediately after verdict, and before the court proceeded to any other business.

32 Cf. W. K. Wimsatt, Jr, 'The Game of Ombre in *The Rape of the Lock*', *RES,* n.s. I (1950), 142.

33 *The Rape of the Lock and Other Poems,* p. 91.

34 *Pope and Human Nature* (Oxford, 1958), p. 255.

35 'The Limits of Allusion in *The Rape of the Lock*', in *Twentieth Century Interpretations,* p. 79. Wasserman, however, in order to derive support from this echo of the *Ars Amatoria,* III. 449–50, for his general

thesis, is forced to interpret it as a reflection on Belinda rather than the Baron.

36 *Aeneid*, VI. 458–60 ('By the stars I swear, by the world above, and whatever is sacred in the grave below, unwillingly, O queen, I parted from your shores').

37 LXVI. 39–41 ('Unwillingly, O queen, I parted from your head, unwillingly, I swear both by you and by your head; by which, if any swear vainly, let him reap a worthy recompense').

38 *The Rape of the Lock and Other Poems*, pp. 91–2.

39 *Correspondence of Pope*, I. 207.

40 *Ibid.*, I. 271–2; cf. p. 269.

41 Quoted in *The Rape of the Lock and Other Poems*, p. 100.

An Epistle
to Dr. Arbuthnot

Pope's own description of *An Epistle to Dr. Arbuthnot* as 'a Sort of
Bill of Complaint, begun many years since, and drawn up by
snatches, as the several Occasions offer'd', has perhaps been instrumental in discouraging critics from paying enough attention
to its unified structure. Certainly its three famous satiric portraits
have often been considered in almost total isolation from the rest
of the poem. In her recently reprinted book on Pope's poetry,
Rebecca P. Parkin, for example, has not only likened the function
of the Atticus and Sporus portraits to that of 'interpolated anecdotes', but listed those of Bufo and Sporus among the means by
which Pope seeks to prevent 'the autobiography of the good man,
the poem's speaker', from degenerating into 'pious fatuity'.[1] Even
Reuben A. Brower, who claims that the *Epistle* is 'a poetic biography', 'the epitome of a satirist's career as Pope saw it', gives no
consideration to its controlling, organic, unity. Concluding that it
is ' "poetic biography" in a rather special sense, a kind of résumé
of modes Pope had perfected while "imitating" Dryden and
Horace', Brower is content to explain its character as an apologia
in the following general terms:[2] 'Like the best of Horace's
Epistles, it is the kind of letter we dream of writing, our own talk

brought to paper without any obvious plan or artifice, yet capable of embracing whatever concerns or amuses us.' Yet directly relevant to its character as an apologia is, as we shall see, its skilfully articulated structure. The three famous satiric portraits occur within a specific context, being framed, so to speak, by the poet's studied, cleverly sustained, self-characterization. And it is the moral validity that attaches to this persona—a validity ultimately confirmed by the implied contrast between the poet-speaker and the satiric portraits themselves—which not only makes their inclusion seem, in absolute terms, defensible, but throws the satire they contain into such high relief.

Though the three famous satirists of imperial Rome all wrote apologies for satire, none of these provides a precise source for Pope's *Epistle to Dr. Arbuthnot*. Despite J. C. Maxwell's contention that Persius's first satire 'comes closer to being a model for Pope's poem than does any other ancient work',[3] its castigation of the contemporary literary scene does not anticipate the ethical question concerning personalized satire which, presumably as a result of his friend Arbuthnot's prompting, so obviously lies at the very heart of Pope's *Epistle*. Arguably of more relevance is the concluding section of the first satire of Horace's second book, the first of his poems to be 'imitated' by Pope. There the Roman poet represents as follows the dialogue between his lawyer-friend and himself:[4]

> TREB. 'Si mala condiderit in quem quis carmina jus est judiciumque'. HOR. Esto siquis *mala*; sed *bona* siquis judice condiderit laudatur *CAESARE*: siquis opprobrijs dignum laceraverit, integer ipse . . .
>
> (82–5)

What Pope's 'translation' of these lines suggests—his irony and supposed fears for personal safety notwithstanding—is that a dis-

tinction may properly be made between mere libel and an altogether more responsible and morally justifiable form of satire:[5]

> P. *Libels* and *Satires*! lawless Things indeed!
> But grave *Epistles*, bringing Vice to light,
> Such as a *King* might read, a *Bishop* write,
> Such as Sir *Robert* would approve—
>
> (150–3)

Yet this parallel between Horace's apologia and Pope's *Epistle* is
merely incidental, for the Roman satirist also states that he will
reply in kind to anyone who attacks him personally:[6]

> nec quisquam noceat cupido mihi pacis! at ille,
> qui me commorit (melius non tangere, clamo),
> flebit et insignis tota cantabitur urbe.
>
> (44–6)

And Pope, in 'translating' these lines, admits that he may be similarly provoked to write satire from such purely personal motives:

> Peace is my dear Delight—not *Fleury*'s more:
> But touch me, and no Minister so sore.
> Who-e'er offends, at some unlucky Time
> Slides into Verse, and hitches in a Rhyme,
> Sacred to Ridicule! his whole Life long,
> And the sad Burthen of some merry Song.
>
> (75–80)

This sentiment is alien to the whole spirit of the *Epistle to Dr.
Arbuthnot*, where the poet-speaker is above all concerned to show
that his satire proceeds from a sincere abhorrence of vice, and not
from a desire to revenge merely personal affronts. The following
couplet is, in fact, entirely representative of the character that
Pope there presents of himself:

> Full ten years slander'd did he once reply?
> Three thousand Suns went down on *Welsted*'s Lye.
>
> (374–5)

The context in which such claims are uttered is very different from anything to be found in classical satire. Lines like, 'I pay my Debts, believe, and say my Pray'rs' (l. 268), or.

> Why am I ask'd, what next shall see the light?
> Heav'ns! was I born for nothing but to write?
> Has Life no Joys for me? or (to be grave)
> Have I no Friend to serve, no Soul to save?
>
> (271-4)

introduce, despite their lightness of touch, a wholly new, explicitly Christian, framework of reference. It was doubtless from a consciousness of the validity of this in an absolute sense that Pope, in his 'Advertisement' to his Horatian 'imitations', sought to justify his own practice as a satirist by citing not only the authority of Horace, but 'the Example of much greater Freedom in so eminent a Divine as Dr. *Donne*'—an 'example' which to him 'seem'd a proof with what Indignation and Contempt a Christian may treat Vice or Folly, in ever so low, or ever so high, a Station'.[7]

The ethical problem that the Christian satirist faced had, in fact, been clearly highlighted by Dryden, who, in his famous *Discourse concerning Satire* (1693), had distinguished between 'lampoons' written from motives of personal revenge and those written from motives of public duty. The former kind troubled him because they so obviously ran counter to the whole principle of Christian charity and 'the plain condition of the forgiveness which we beg' in saying the Lord's Prayer. But he found no difficulty in stating that 'the second reason which may justify a poet when he writes against a particular person . . . is when he is become a public nuisance'. And Dryden adds: ' 'Tis an action of virtue to make examples of vicious men. . . . The first reason was only an excuse for revenge; but this second is absolutely of a poet's office to perform.'[8]

That Pope could, when it suited him, display a familiarity with the terms of Dryden's argument may be taken for granted. In *A Letter to a Noble Lord*, his projected prose reply to Lord Hervey's scurrilous attack on him in *An Epistle to a Doctor of Divinity from a*

Nobleman at Hampton Court (1733), he had implied his opponent's utter want of Christian charity:[9]

> I cannot but think the worthy and *discreet clergyman* himself will agree, it is *improper*, nay *unchristian*, to expose the *personal* defects of our brother: that both such perfect forms as yours, and such unfortunate ones as mine, proceed from the hand of the same *Maker*; who *fashioneth his Vessels* as he pleaseth, and that it is not from their *shape* we can tell whether they are made for *honour* or *dishonour*. In a word, he would teach you Charity to your greatest enemies; of which number, my Lord, I cannot be reckon'd, since, tho' a Poet, I was never your flatterer.

Pope's verse reply, the Sporus portrait of his *Epistle to Dr. Arbuthnot*, has been attributed by John Butt, the Twickenham editor to its author's 'quivering resentment' at Hervey's attacks on him.[10] Yet such a reading not only obscures the fact that the poem's three famous satiric portraits may all be regarded as exposing manifest vice and corruption, but fails to appreciate the deftness of Pope's wit in turning the arguments against personalized satire so decidedly to his own advantage. Though he had previously replied to Arbuthnot by saying he had taken to heart his friend's advice 'concerning avoiding Ill-will from writing Satyr',[11] it is the character he presents of himself in the poem that makes any assumption of malice on his part seem so wide of the mark. From the outset the poet-speaker shows an exemplary forbearance in dealing with the horde of foolish poetasters and criticasters that prove so persistently vexing. And this forbearance, in immediately putting the purity of his motives as a satirist beyond any dispute, plays an important part in the essential logic of the poem's progression. Indeed, his forbearance is such as to recall not merely Dryden's definition of 'urbanity' as 'well-mannered wit', but the same author's description of 'good nature' as ' beneficence and candour [i.e. kindliness] . . . which of necessity will give allowance to the failings of others', and as, in short, 'the most god-like commendation of a man'.[12]

Whereas Pope, in his first 'imitation' of Horace, had explained his predisposition to satire by saying, 'Fools rush into my Head, and so I write' (l. 14), in the *Epistle to Dr. Arbuthnot* he represents himself as willing to do all he can to avoid having fools thrust themselves upon his consciousness. The opening of the poem does not, as has been suggested, constitute a 'tirade';[13] nor is the tone here one of 'scorn and rage'.[14] In stressing his urbane detachment at Twickenham from the contemporary world of witlings and flatterers, the poet-speaker gives expression to, at most, a certain wry exasperation. Far from moving him to satire, the mindless provocation of such people merely prompts him to have his door shut against them. And even though the invasion of his privacy still goes on, his reaction to this is expressed with a witty exaggeration indicative of almost good-natured tolerance:

> What *Drop* or *Nostrum* can this Plague remove?
> Or which must end me, a Fool's Wrath or Love?
> A dire Dilemma! either way I'm sped,
> If Foes, they write, if Friends, they read me dead.
>
> (29-32)

His tolerance becomes obvious when, asked his opinion of some worthless stuff, he is prepared to 'sit with sad Civility' and read 'With honest anguish, and an aking head' (l. 38). Even unfair attacks on him personally would appear to call forth his benevolence rather than his sarcasm:

> Yet then did *Gildon* draw his venal quill;
> I wish'd the man a dinner, and sate still:
> Yet then did *Dennis* rave in furious fret;
> I never answer'd, I was not in debt.
>
> (151-4)

He is only 'glad of a quarrel' (l. 67) when he can thus be rid of one of the witlings as the result of a suggestion that would have compromised his own honesty. And consistently he owns—though, of course, with a certain witty ambiguity—a disposition to ignore the attacks of others:

> Were others angry? I excus'd them too;
> Well might they rage; I gave them but their due.
>
> (173-4)

The wit rather than the avowed benevolence seems uppermost in lines 189-90:

> All these, my modest Satire bad *translate*
> And own'd, that nine such Poets made a *Tate*.

Yet if the earlier version of these lines—

> Should modest Satire bid all these *translate*,
> And own that nine such Poets make a *Tate*—

could not be printed after Pope had written *The Dunciad*, it is interesting to note that he is still concerned to represent his satire as 'modest'.

Given Thomas E. Maresca's perceptive analysis of the poem's mythopoeia, it would, in fact, seem entirely logical to expect that its author should have cast himself in the role of Christian satirist. In a study which has greatly enriched our appreciation of the poem, Maresca argues that Pope's various allusions 'establish the symbolic identity of literary and theological offence in the cosmos of his poem'. He notes that 'the sin of the poetasters is at once poetic and theological', that the poem's 'dialectic of works' distinguishes 'Pope's meritorious poetic works from the chaotic deeds of the dunces', and that in the Sporus portrait Pope's satire becomes 'the divine weapon, the Ithuriel's spear, which exposes and punishes this literary manifestation of the Christian's eternal enemy'.[15] Accordingly, whenever in the initial section the poet's tone becomes indignant, it is to be understood that he is speaking in his assumed role of Christian satirist rather than in order to avenge merely personal affronts. Presumably in such instances the object of his attack will represent, or at least suggest, such a perversion of Christian values that no doubt will be cast on his own honesty of purpose.

The first occasion on which the poet-speaker assumes a tone of righteous indignation (ll. 69–108) is, even so, imagined as provoking some degree of remonstration from his poetical friend. When he introduces the example of the legendary King Midas, he is urged (as Pope was by Arbuthnot's letter of the previous July) to avoid particularized satire out of consideration for his own safety. As Maresca has pointed out, Midas is to be associated with the dunces (in having obtained his asses ears by preferring Pan's music to Apollo's), and especially with England's fatuous, boorish, culturally illiterate, George II.[16] Yet, though the poetical friend's warning would thus seem to be timely, the poet-speaker justifiably ignores it. The true satirist must have the courage to expose vice and folly in whatever station they appear. Dunces are, anyway, so congenitally impervious to criticism that the poet-speaker certainly does not impugn his own humanity in attacking them. Thus he ingeniously anticipates any charge of 'cruelty' on his part by using the example of Codrus to demonstrate that 'No creature smarts so little as a fool' (l. 84). Moreover, his particular animus is rightly reserved for the flatterer:

> A Fool quite angry is quite innocent;
> Alas! 'tis ten times worse when they *repent*.
>
> (107–8)

The animal imagery of the poem, which may be said to begin with the reference to King Midas,[17] a perversion of God's representative on earth, conveys within a very few lines an anticipation of that greater perversion of the human and godlike which, at its most venomous, arouses feelings not just of repugnance but of intense loathing. The 'bite' of the angry fool is greatly to be preferred to the 'slaver' of the flatterer:

> One Flatt'rer's worse than all;
> Of all mad Creatures, if the Learn'd are right,
> It is the Slaver kills, and not the Bite.
>
> (104–6)

Here, as has been aptly suggested, Pope is alluding to the description of the critic in *A Tale of A Tub*: '. . . there is a Serpent that wants Teeth, and consequently cannot bite, but if its Vomit . . . happens to fall upon any Thing, a certain Rottenness or Corruption ensues'.[18] Thus these lines of the *Epistle to Dr. Arbuthnot* clearly look forward to the later attack on the court-flatterer and serpent-tempter Sporus, in whose portrait the satire of the poem reaches its climax.

The poet-speaker also assumes a tone of righteous indignation when, naming Bentley and Theobald, he later becomes outspoken against verbal critics. This time, however, his poetical friend enters no imagined objection since these were figures whom neither Arbuthnot nor any other enlightened contemporary would have dreamt of defending. Not only were such critics guilty of a gross disservice to the classics of English literature by mangling the noble work of a Shakespeare or Milton, but their pedantry was characterized, in the words of David Mallet's poem *On Verbal Criticism*, by both 'pride and dulness' (l. 185). And given that the contemporary reader of the *Epistle to Dr. Arbuthnot* would have been fully aware of the pride to be associated with their whole undertaking, Pope's lines anticipate not only the explicit mention of 'pride' (according to Christian ethics, the cardinal sin) in the following verse-paragraph, but also the searing indictments of this vice in the portraits that follow.

Despite these thematic links with the rest of the poem, the tone of its initial section nevertheless provides an expressive contrast rather than a comparison with what follows. The poet has been able to affect a truly Christian forbearance towards the relatively innocuous witlings because their 'pride' is displayed in conjunction with their own indisputable 'emptiness' (l. 177). But he cannot afford to be in the least indulgent towards an Atticus, a Bufo or a Sporus. Their besetting sin is also pride; and they are possessed of a far greater genius for evil. Thus in his role of Christian satirist he is now obliged to speak out strongly, pointing to the very real threat that they present to the virtuous citizen and genuine poet.

When Arbuthnot enjoined his friend to 'continue that noble *Disdain* and *Abhorrence* of Vice, which you seem naturally endu'd with, but still with a due regard to your own Safety; and study more to reform than chastise', Pope replied by saying that, though willing to attempt more generalized satire, he was in some doubt concerning its ultimate efficacy:[19]

> I would indeed do it with more restrictions, and less person- ally; it is more agreeable to my nature, which those who know it not are greatly mistaken in: But General Satire in Times of General Vice has no force, and is no Punishment: People have ceas'd to be ashamed of it when so many are joined with them; and tis only by hunting One or two from the Herd that any Examples can be made.

In the 'Advertisement' to his poem, however, Pope states that he has 'for the most part' omitted the names of those satirized out of deference to his friend's request. His practice in the poem repre- sents, in fact, a felicitous compromise that avoids any appearance of malevolence on his part at the same time as it ensures that specific examples of the 'vice' of pride will be unambiguously exposed. Doubtless Pope remembered the point made in his earlier 'imitation' of Horace:

> F. A hundred smart in *Timon* and in *Balaam*:
> The fewer still you name, you wound the more;
> *Bond* is but one, but *Harpax* is a Score.
>
> (42-4)

As a creative artist he must have recognized the advantage to be gained from satiric portraiture that had an applicability beyond the narrowly particular, and the use to which symbolic names might be put. Addison, moreover, had been dead for many years, and there could have seemed little point in not substituting the nicely ironic pseudonym Atticus, which, as the name of Cicero's correspondent and friend, would have recalled a very different 'exemplar of the retired life—an ideal of self-sufficiency and contemplation'.[20] Yet while Pope uses names which seem clearly to indicate that he is not indulging in a personal attack on individuals, the effectiveness of his satire is increased by such details as suggest concrete examples of what he is concerned to expose. Certain references facilitate the identification of Atticus with Addison and of Sporus with Hervey. Moreover, though no individual patron sat for the Bufo portrait, some of its lines seem to apply to either Bubb Dodington or the Earl of Halifax. The result is that, as satire, it becomes seemingly more credible and trenchant. Indeed, while giving to his portraits a mythopoeic dimension, Pope draws them with a pen practised in etching the vividly actual.

The first portrait, seemingly drawn more in sorrow than in anger, represents the perversion of all those virtues that the reader has come to attribute to the poet-speaker himself. Atticus welcomes the applause of sycophants, harbours ill-will towards kindred merit, and shows that his apparent urbanity is vitiated by pride. The balanced precision of Pope's language—

> Willing to wound, and yet afraid to strike,
> Just hint a fault, and hesitate dislike—
>
> (203–4)

brilliantly captures the cold, sly, studied reserve, indicative at once of cowardice and malice. In fact the malice is such as undermines the values, and hence the confidence, of the whole republic of letters. With a nice irony Pope turns against Atticus the same criticism that had been levelled against himself when Addison, in *Spectator* 253, had lamented the want in the author of *An Essay on Criticism* of that 'candour and ingenuity' [i.e. kindliness and ingenuousness] for which Denham had praised Fletcher:

> I need not raise
> Trophies to thee from other men's dispraise;
> Nor is thy fame on lesser ruins built,

Nor needs thy juster title the foul guilt
Of eastern Kings, who to secure their reign
Must have their brothers, sons, and kindred slain.

Like the eastern ruler ('the *Turk*') who kills off his immediate relatives in order to enjoy a secure possession of the throne, Atticus dispatches those brother authors who might prove rivals, surrounding himself instead with obsequious and foolish flatterers. In view of the contempt, jealousy and hatred that he is said to feel towards his peers (ll. 199–200), it may not be too fanciful to suggest a parallel with *Paradise Lost*, where Satan, the author of all pride and malevolence, is at the beginning of the second book likened to an eastern potentate. Certainly the pride that Atticus so clearly displays not only links him with Bufo and the explicitly Satanic aspects of Sporus, but contrasts sharply with the forbearance, and even charity, that the poet-speaker himself displays. Consistently with his assumed character, Pope expresses his concern that such genuine talents should be so ignobly misapplied. Indeed, the objectivity of his judgment of Atticus—which in an earlier version of these lines had been assured by the explicit reference to 'heaven' ('What pity, Heav'n, if such a Man there be')— is in the later poem confirmed by the whole context in which it is uttered.

Pope's portrait of the worthless patron Bufo furthers both the theme of a pride that perverts the whole republic of letters, and the developing contrast between the character of the poet-speaker and those he satirizes. *Bufo* is Latin for 'toad', a creature not only traditionally regarded as 'ugly and venomous' (*As You Like It*, II. i. 13), but associated with pride, and with Satan himself. In *Troilus and Cressida*, for example, Ajax says: 'I do hate a proud man as I do hate the engend'ring of toads' (II. iii 144). Pope's opening lines illustrate the thoroughly grotesque ugliness of the state of contemporary letters by presenting patron Bufo as both the god of the modern Parnassus and the modern Maecenas ('*Horace* and he went hand in hand in song', l. 234).[21] According to Elder Olson, the purpose of this portrait is 'to show the kind of character to whom "the Castalian state" would be desirable, to provide an object for the contempt of Pope, and so to disclaim any similar ambition' on his part.[22] But its purpose is also to underline the really pernicious consequences attendant on a pride capable of being 'puff'd' by every poetaster's 'quill' (l. 232). Toad Bufo, in perverting the god-like role of patron, has polluted the very source of poetry itself: his pride is responsible not only for an undiscerning encouragement of those worthless authors prepared to gratify his own self-esteem, but also for his unjust neglect of the poet of genuine merit unable to stoop to such base flattery. Here, too, Pope gives concreteness to his satire by invoking Dryden as his example of the writer of genius unjustly neglected by such a patron as Bufo:

> *Dryden* alone (what wonder?) came not nigh,
> *Dryden* alone escap'd this judging eye:
> But still the Great have kindness in reserve,
> He help'd to bury whom he help'd to starve.
>
> (245-8)

The first of these lines applies, of course, to neither Dodington nor Halifax, to the latter of whom Dryden wrote asking for his encouragement in a translation of Homer, and from whom he had received a subscription for his Virgil. But the last line doubtless refers to Halifax's intention—which came to nothing—of erecting a monument to the poet's memory in Westminster Abbey. And this stinging allusion may be taken in conjunction with other lines in the poem to illustrate both the meanness and the honest author's necessary independence of contemporary patronage. That the poet-speaker thinks of himself as Dryden's lineal descendant is clear from the earlier passage in which he describes the encouragement his own work received from that group of writers and men of eminence in the state who were 'great *Dryden*'s friends before' (l. 141); 'all these', as Pope explains in a note, 'were Patrons or Admirers of Mr. *Dryden*'. They are therefore to be distinguished from that more numerous body of 'the *Great*' which let Gay's 'genius' die 'neglected' (ll. 255ff.). Perhaps Pope, in drawing the Bufo portrait, remembered his own early experience of reading to an inattentive and opinionated Halifax his translation of the first few books of the *Iliad*.[23] Certainly the virtuous independence to which he gives expression in the *Epistle to Dr. Arbuthnot* may serve to remind us that so large were the profits from his translations of Homer as to make him independent of the traditional form of literary patronage. But not all men of genius had been as fortunate as Pope. The lines on Gay are the most moving in the poem; and though, in the words of the Twickenham editor, 'the only "neglect" which Gay's genius suffered was the absence of political patronage, which he had done nothing to deserve',[24] it should be obvious that Pope, in giving a different emphasis by this poignant mention of his friend, highlights the self-interest of the contemporary statesman and patron who gave employment to the pens of dunces and courted the attention of flatterers (cf. ll. 249ff.).

The pride-flattery theme reaches its climax in the last of the three portraits, where the characterization of Sporus serves to remind us that his prototype Satan was both the author of all pride and the original flatterer of mankind. Characterized in the Satanic attitudes of 'toad' and 'reptile', this Court-eunuch, who so obviously has the Queen's ear, is in a position to infect with his toad-like venom the very source of power itself:

> Or at the Ear of *Eve*, familiar Toad,
> Half Froth, half Venom, spits himself abroad,
> In Puns, or Politicks, or Tales, or Lyes . . .
>
> (319–21)

That such 'venom' is an insidiously corrupting and corrosive force may be inferred from the earlier reference to the flatterer's 'slaver' in a passage which, together with its Swiftian allusion, anticipates Sporus's ultimate identification with 'the creature fundamentally evil and the prime agent of corruption'.[25] And it is for this reason, I suggest, that Pope's description excites a degree of loathing unmatched by anything even in *The Dunciad*. Whereas the longer poem, which significantly numbers *Mac Flecknoe* among its literary ancestors, is primarily a phantasmagoric representation of the forces of anti-culture by a great comic genius, in the Sporus portrait Pope depicts a grotesque malformation of the human with a sinister potential for perverting, Satan-like, the whole of society.

In his unnatural capering and reptilean abjectness, Sporus represents the complete emasculation of all virtue. And this is but the most obvious of those points of contrast between him and the poet-speaker which contribute immeasurably to the coherence and unity of the *Epistle* as a whole. The latter claims 'That, if he pleas'd, he pleas'd by manly ways' (l. 337)—by behaviour totally unlike that of the 'vile Antithesis' Sporus. He now makes explicit and emphatic the standards he has sought to live by; and because these are so different from what has previously been described, his virtue appears neither unctuous nor complacent. In particular, he invites the reader to consider his behaviour as a man and his more mature work as expressions of the same personality:

> That Flatt'ry, ev'n to Kings, he held a shame,
> And thought a Lye in Verse or Prose the same:
> That not in Fancy's Maze he wander'd long,
> But stoop'd to Truth, and moraliz'd his song:
> That not for Fame, but Virtue's better end . . .
>
> (338–42)

Doubtless Pope was here referring not merely to his *Essay on Man*, in which he praises Bolingbroke as the 'guide, philosopher, and friend' (IV. 390) who had been instrumental in suggesting to him more serious themes, but also to his satires, and especially those *Epistles* which, originally conceived as part of his 'system of ethics in the Horatian way',[26] were intended to have a place in his proposed *magnum opus*. In fact this passage, coming as it does immediately after the Sporus portrait, reminds us that the morally instructive aims of the satirist—especially of the poet whose satires are avowedly 'grave Epistles', not 'libels'—are to be regarded as directly antithetical to the insidious aims of the flatterer. Like the original Serpent-tempter who misled man's first parents concerning their proper nature, the flatterer represents men in a false light by pandering to their self-esteem, and thereby encourages the worst of all vices, pride. The purpose of the satirist is, on the contrary, to show men plainly what they are really like by constantly exposing vice and folly. Thus it seems appropriate that Pope's reference in this passage to his later work should be taken to include his satires as well as his *Essay on Man*. For the true satirist, as well as for the philosophical poet, 'the proper study of mankind is man'.

Yet Sporus was a libeller as well as a flatterer, and in this respect, too, Pope's characterization of Hervey is to be sharply contrasted with the character that he consciously presents of himself. Though the view attributed to the poetical friend would suggest that the 'butterfly' Sporus does not warrant the satirist's serious attention, Pope was peculiarly aware that 'this Bug with gilded wings' could 'sting' as well as 'stink' (ll. 309–10). Thus he had written to Hervey in *A Letter to a Noble Lord*: 'Above all, your Lordship will be careful not to wrong my *Moral Character* with THOSE [i.e. the King and Queen] under whose *Protection* I live, and through whose *Lenity* alone I can live with Comfort.'[27] In his *Epistle*, however, he merely refers to

> The Whisper that to Greatness still too near,
> Perhaps, yet vibrates on his SOVEREIGN's Ear
>
> (356–7)

as but one of the misrepresentations of his character he has had to endure. There his satire on Hervey is in every way consistent with his remark in an earlier letter to Arbuthnot that he will consult his own safety only 'so far as I think becomes a prudent man; but not so far as to omit any thing which I think becomes an honest one'.[28] Thus, in holding up the waspishness and 'florid Impotence' (l. 317) of this figure to such killing ridicule, the poet-speaker is also motivated by his unfailing opposition, as satirist, to those who read

> but with a Lust to mis-apply,
> Make Satire a Lampoon, and Fiction, Lye.
>
> (301–2)

That Pope here had Hervey especially in mind is suggested not just by what follows, but by the preceding couplet as well:

Who to the *Dean* and *silver Bell* can swear,
And sees at *Cannons* what was never there.

Hervey, Pope's arch-slanderer or lampooner at this period, had impugned the poet's good nature by repeating in his scurrilous *Verses addressed to the Imitator of Horace* (1733) the common, but quite unfounded, charge that Pope had maliciously satirized the Duke of Chandos—a man to whom it was thought he had reason to be grateful—in his description of Timon's villa.[29]

In marked contrast to the insidious malevolence of a Sporus are those virtues intended to prove the speaker's moral fitness for the task of Christian satirist. Disclaiming any inherent disposition to satire, he represents himself as naturally tender-hearted, slow to realize (much less return) personal affronts, and a friend even to an enemy's distress. Yet his reply (ll. 361ff.) to his poetical friend's last imagined objection also makes it clear that, while prepared to allow slanderous and scurrilous attacks on himself to go un-answered, he is courageously determined to expose vice, whatever the social rank of the person meriting his censure. And that these defences of both his satire and his character should have become the very polarities of his argument invites us to view his conduct as a satirist in the light of those principles that had previously been enunciated by Dryden. Of course Pope continually makes poetic capital out of the argument on which this apologia turns: his wit clearly manifests itself in his being able to write a poem that demolishes a lot besides the three central figures at the same time as it defends his assumed role as satirist according to unimpeach-able moral standards. The carefully cultivated persona not only serves to enhance his own character, but cleverly shows up the witlings and others for what they are. In fact Pope's technique is akin to *occupatio*: his rhetorical ingenuity is such that his poet-speaker is allowed to enumerate all sorts of affronts under the guise of a professed willingness to ignore them.

At this point Pope felicitously extends what is ostensibly the autobiographical content of his poem to reinforce further its constant display of virtuous intentions. According to the strictest possible interpretation of a Christian's duty, the moral excellence of the speaker's parents is clearly beyond question:

> That Father held it for a rule
> It was a Sin to call our Neighbour Fool,
> That harmless Mother thought no Wife a Whore.
>
> (382–4)

This description of his father explicitly recalls Christ's injunction in Matthew, V. 22:[30]

> But I say unto you, That whosoever is angry with his brother without a cause shall be in danger of judgment: and whosoever shall say to his brother, Raca, shall be in danger of the council: but whosoever shall say, Thou Fool, shall be in danger of hell fire.

If the son, notwithstanding his avowed tolerance towards the witlings and those who have attacked him personally, does not walk 'innoxious thro' his Age' (l. 395) with quite the same kind of virtuous detachment as had his father, then this is to be attributed to the fact that he has been born a poet (cf. ll. 125 ff.), and thus, given sufficient 'cause', must assume the moral responsibility of being a satirist. The description of his mother, who is obviously prepared to carry her Christian charity to almost inordinate lengths, invites comparison with a couplet that had occurred several lines previously:

> To please a *Mistress*, One aspers'd his life;
> He lash'd him not, but let her be his *Wife*.
>
> (376–7)

Pope is here saying—though without mentioning any names—
that he forbore to satirize William Windham who, having col-
laborated with Hervey and Lady Mary Wortley Montagu in the
Verses addressed to the Imitator of Horace, had become the Countess
of Delorain's second husband. Moreover, with respect to this
lady, Pope was very likely reporting what was common knowledge rather than obliquely resorting to libel. Though we do not
know whether she was Windham's mistress before he married her,
it does not seem improbable given that she was soon to become,
in Hervey's colourful language, the 'whore' of George II.[31] Indeed, Pope would seem to have been letting her off lightly in this
passing allusion. He had previously satirized her as Delia in his
first 'imitation' of Horace: 'Slander or Poyson, dread from *Delia's*
Rage' (l. 81). Nor does this earlier charge seem to have been unjust. As Maid of Honour to Queen Caroline, she was supposed to
have tried to poison another maid of honour; while according to
Hervey himself, she was 'very dangerous', possessed of 'a lying
tongue and a false heart', and always busy about some 'sad work'.[32]

The speaker's description of his parents is not just a defence of
them but a defence of himself as well: his 'generosity' (to use the
word in its now obsolete sense) cannot be established in any other
way. As a defence of his moral character, it therefore reinforces
his earlier appeal to the judgment of those men who, 'great
Dryden's friends before', not only had encouraged his youthful
work, but themselves represent the touchstone of posterity:

> From these the world will judge of Men and Books,
> Not from the *Burnets*, *Oldmixons*, and *Cooks*.
>
> (145–6)

This assumed connection between the literary and the moral, itself a commonplace of the humanist tradition, forms the basis of
Pope's defence of the satirist's role: the poet must needs establish
his good faith by demonstrating that only the most honourable
motives prompt his satire. And that the poet-speaker of Pope's
Epistle effectively demonstrates this is finally suggested by the
measure of agreement that, at the end of the poem, apparently

exists between him and his poetical friend. This friend's supposed presence as interlocutor functions as 'both a satiric point of reference, and a guarantee of Pope's good character';[33] and though he is earlier imagined as opposing particularized satire, he seems, as the poem progresses, to show a growing acquiescence in the point-of-view put forward, and to become increasingly convinced of the moral validity of the motives to satire there displayed. Moreover, the tone of the final verse-paragraph also suggests the poet-speaker's humble confidence in the honesty of his own endeavours. Thus he is prepared to acknowledge that 'the rest belongs to Heav'n'; and these are, significantly, the last words he utters.

Notes

1 *The Poetic Workmanship of Alexander Pope* (New York, 1966, reprinted), pp. 149, 151–2.
2 *Alexander Pope: The Poetry of Allusion* (Oxford, 1963, 2nd rev. ed.), pp. 294, 296.
3 'Pope's Use of the First Satire of Persius in the *Epistle to Dr. Arbuthnot*', *NQ*, CCXIII (1968), 207.
4 I have quoted here from the text that Pope himself gives of this Horatian satire. ('Treb. "If a man write bad verses against another, there is a right of action and redress by law". Hor. To be sure, if the verses are bad. But what if a man write good verses, and Caesar's judgment approve? If, blameless himself, he has torn someone to pieces who deserves abuse?')
5 Cf. *Correspondence of Pope*, ed. Sherburn, III. 366, Pope to Swift (April 1733): 'You call your satires, Libels; I would rather call my satires, Epistles: They will consist more of morality than wit, and grow graver, which you will call duller'.
6 'Let no man injure me, a lover of peace! But if one stir me up ("Better not touch me!" I shout), he shall smart for it and have his name sung up and down the town.'
7 *Imitations of Horace*, ed. John Butt (London, 1961 reprint), p. 3.
8 *John Dryden: Of Dramatic Poesy and Other Critical Essays*, ed. George Watson (London, 1962), II. 126–7.
9 *The Works of Alexander Pope*, ed. William Warburton (London, 1766 ed.), VIII. 268.
10 *Imitations of Horace*, ed. Butt, p. xix.

11 *Correspondence of Pope*, III. 428.

12 *Of Dramatic Poesy and Other Critical Essays*, II. 74-5, 122. Watson glosses 'candour' as 'purity', 'integrity', but it seems to me far more likely that Dryden was using the word here in the sense of 'kindliness', 'sweetness of temper'—clearly the sense in which he had used it in the Dedication of his *Annus Mirabilis*. It may be noted that the periodical essayists Steele and Addison had also insisted that true satire should not be ill-natured. Cf. *Tatler* 242, and *Spectator* 23 (where Addison regards satire as a 'breech of charity') and 355.

13 Parkin, *The Poetic Workmanship of Alexander Pope*, p. 150.

14 Penelope Curtis, 'Pope the Good Augustan', *Melbourne Critical Review*, VII (1964), 46.

15 *Pope's Horatian Poems* (Columbus, Ohio, 1966), pp. 75-6, 79.

16 *Ibid.*, pp. 87-9.

17 I find myself unable to agree with Elias F. Mengel, Jr, 'Patterns of Imagery in Pope's *Arbuthnot*', in *Essential Articles for the Study of Alexander Pope*, ed. Maynard Mack (London, 1968, rev. ed.), pp. 567-8, who detects animal imagery earlier in the poem at ll. 3ff. and 7ff. Though the 'Dog-star' was popularly associated with madness (as in Pope's lines), it did not derive its name from the madness caused by dogs; nor does Pope's description of the madness of these poetasters suggest that they are being characterized as dogs. Mengel claims that Pope's diction in ll. 7ff. '. . . suggests a mad swarm of insects descending on the villa, the sudden swoop of hornets or a plague of locusts'; but the syntactical arrangement of Pope's phrases suggests that 'thro' my Grot they glide' is to be taken as referring to those who 'by water . . . renew the charge'. An adequate gloss on these lines is provided by the opening couplet of Pope's *Verses on a Grotto by the River Thames at Twickenham*:

> Thou who shalt stop, where *Thames'* translucent Wave
> Shines a broad Mirrour thro' the shadowy Cave . . .

18 See Jo Allen Bradham, 'Pope's *An Epistle to Dr. Arbuthnot*, 104-106', *The Explicator*, XXVI (1968), item 50.

19 *Correspondence of Pope*, III. 417, 423.

20 Maresca, *Pope's Horatian Poems*, p. 84.

21 Cf. *Imitations of Horace*, ed. Butt, p. 112n.

22 'Rhetoric and the Appreciation of Pope', *MP*, XXXVII (1939-1940), 28.

23 See *Joseph Spence: Observations, Anecdotes, and Characters of Books and Men*, ed. James M. Osborn (Oxford, 1966), I. 87-8.

24 *Imitations of Horace*, p. 362.

25 Bradham, 'Pope's *An Epistle to Dr. Arbuthnot*, 104-6'.

26 *Correspondence of Pope*, III. 81.

27 *Works of Pope*, ed. Warburton (1766 ed.), VIII. 279.
28 *Correspondence of Pope*, III. 419-20.
29 See *Epistles to Several Persons (Moral Essays)*, ed. F. W. Bateson (London, Twickenham ed., 1961, 2nd ed.), pp. 170ff.; cf. J. V. Guerinot, *Pamphlet Attacks on Alexander Pope 1711-14* (London, 1969), p. 227.
30 Cited by Maresca, *Pope's Horatian Poems*, pp. 103-4.
31 See Maynard Mack, 'A Couplet in the *Epistle to Dr. Arbuthnot*', *TLS*, 2 September 1939, p. 515.
32 Cf. *Imitations of Horace*, p. 367.
33 P. Dixon, 'The Theme of Friendship in the *Epistle to Dr. Arbuthnot*', *English Studies*, XLIV (1963), 192.

London

Though an enlightened reappraisal of Johnson's poetry has taken place during the past few decades, critics still tend to refer rather slightingly to his first great poem *London*. Except in T. S. Eliot's notable essay,[1] this 'imitation' in the Augustan manner of Juvenal's famous satire on Rome has received far less than its due. Joseph Wood Krutch has dismissed it as 'a skilfully executed exercise';[2] while Sydney Roberts, too, has spoken of it as 'in form . . . a Latinist's exercise'.[3] Critics have, in fact, remained blind to the poem that Johnson actually wrote because of their preconceived notion of what he might have been expected to write. Accordingly, they have viewed Juvenal's third satire as a rather Procrustean model, instead of recognizing that *London* has its own original and distinctive theme, and is an undeniably impressive poem in its own right.

What has seemed to critics especially uncharacteristic of Johnson is his treatment of the contrast between city and country which is

found in his Latin original. James Boswell took this to exemplify
its author's 'prejudices as a "true-born Englishman"', not only
against foreign countries, but against Ireland and Scotland';[4] yet
this is, to say the least, a curious reading of the couplet,

> For who would leave, unbrib'd, Hibernia's land,
> Or change the rocks of Scotland for the Strand?
>
> (9–10)

Later critics, though rightly reading these lines at their face-
value, have nevertheless been perplexed to find this sentiment
uttered by one who found the metropolis such a congenial home.
Hugh Walker writes: 'With the knowledge we now have of
Johnson's opinions and likings, we are disturbed in *London* by
praises of the country as a setting for life far preferable to the
Strand'.[5] And Krutch finds 'the conventional contrast between the
country and the city . . . little short of fantastic coming as it does
from a man who was as completely and contentedly urban as any
one who ever lived'.[6] H. M. Currie has sought to explain this dis-
crepancy by stating that Johnson '. . . adopted in his *London* a pose
and advanced views alien to his own, following, for example, the
denunciation of the town which he had found in the Latin
original'.[7] But the truth is not so simple as this, for the attitude to
the country expressed in Johnson's poem is, as we shall see, very
different from that expressed in Juvenal's third satire. The critic
of *London* should primarily be concerned to ask what creative use
the English poet made of the contrast he found in his original.

Mary Lascelles has noted that the Latin poem assumes the form
of a dialogue between friends in which Umbricius, 'playing the
part of Juvenal's well-wisher, takes leave of him with the advice:
"Do as I am doing. Cut loose from Rome, and live by yourself in
the country" .' Yet, as she rightly observes, 'we are sensible of an
unspoken commentary', for the poet himself has no intention of
taking this advice:[8]

His real theme is not country pleasures but the mingled
attraction and repulsion exercised by the great cosmopolitan

city, and Umbricius' leave-taking is merely an occasion for a
denunciation of all that displeases him in Roman life.

Juvenal's pose is ironic, and the irony is pervasive from the outset: *ego vel Prochytam praepono Suburae*. There is no place *tam
miserum, tam solum* ('so dismal, so lonely')—not even the desolate
little island of Procida—which the poet does not pretend to prefer
to one of the chief, though noisiest, streets of Rome.

Juvenal's city-country antithesis, then, is not a simple one. The
metropolis, despite its discomforts and dangers, acts like a magnet
on the poet, who is therefore unable to exalt a life of retirement in
the country as a real alternative to life in the city. Johnson, on the
other hand, whole-heartedly condemns the corrupt city and praises
the country. The reader of *London* should not be misled by the fact
that its author was later a confirmed city-dweller, but recognize instead that the poem's contrast between country and city is rhetorical, with its own special validity and point. As poet Johnson
shows good reason for depicting life in the country as a desirable
and even necessary alternative to life in the city.

As a poem on the evils of city life, *London* exploits a familiar
theme. Johnson, however, gives individual expression to this,
not only by displaying a *saeva indignatio* at times as intense as any
in English poetry, but also by developing this theme within a
specific historical context. Though from the outset the city is described as a place of 'malice, rapine, accident', of physical danger
and moral corruption, *London* is not a topical poem merely in the
sense that it mentions fires, falling houses, fell attorneys and female atheists among the social evils to be found in the eighteenth-
century capital. It is also a topical poem in the sense that it satirizes the measures of a particular government and the corruption
which that government was thought to have fostered. Its composition coincided, in Boswell's words, with 'that ferment against
the Court and the ministry, which some years after ended in the
downfall of Sir Robert Walpole'.[9] Thus the Oxford editors of the
poem have pointed out that Johnson's 'antipathy to Walpole's
administration is given free scope in the allusions to excise, the
abuse of pensions, the tyranny of the licensing laws, and the

servitude of a thoughtless age'.[10] As Donald J. Greene remarks in his book on Johnson's politics, such allusions echoed 'the merest commonplaces of opposition propaganda'.[11] Walpole was accused at this time of corruption at home and appeasement abroad. In the domestic sphere Johnson deplored both excise and a system of political pensions which, he feared, would inevitably lead to a corrupt system of government through dependants, thereby reducing Britain to a nation of sycophants. And Walpole's foreign policy was imagined as having similarly dangerous consequences in pursuing a servile attitude towards France and Spain. These countries were Britain's traditional enemies. With the Seven Years War still unfought, the threat of France as Britain's natural rival was never far from Johnson's thoughts. He made the point emphatically not only in his poem, by picturing a capital overrun with Frenchmen, but also in his *Marmor Norfolciense* of the following year, in his report of the Lords debate (13 February 1741) on the motion to remove Walpole, and in his *Introduction to the Political State of Great-Britain*, published in the first number of the *Literary Magazine* for 1756.[12]

Though Johnson's strictures on city life have been dismissed as a 'masterpiece of the higgledy-piggledy',[13] *London* is far more deftly organized than such criticism allows. Indeed, it may even be defended as satisfying Dryden's preference for 'unity of theme, or subject' in satire. Consistently with the kind of unity that arises 'naturally from one subject, as it is diversely treated, in the several subordinate branches of it, all relating to the chief',[14] the political allusions cited above remain not merely incidental, but contribute significantly to the poem's overall theme. By a clever use of rhetorical patterning, Johnson places side by side the reprehensible measures of the government and the moral and even physical degeneracy of the nation—the result being that *London*, far more than its Latin original, takes on the breadth and significance of a political satire.

Johnson gives a decidedly political slant to his satire in a number of ways: by linking social and political immorality in the city; by contrasting an inglorious present with a glorious past; and by extolling the country as the home of the 'true' (though 'harrass'd')

Briton (ll. 8, 47). In a given passage these motifs will often be found to overlap; and it is therefore impossible to discuss any of them in strict isolation. Indeed, the city-country antithesis, in which all of them find various expression, becomes, so to speak, a controlling metaphor containing the poem's essentially political theme.

Thales, the poetical friend in *London*, awaits transport to the country at its threshold Greenwich—a spot which, as the birth-place of Elizabeth, reminds both him and his companion of a former race of monarchs, the defeat of the Armada, and a very different foreign policy towards Spain,

> Ere masquerades debauch'd, excise oppress'd,
> Or English honour grew a standing jest.
>
> (29–30)

And this juxtaposition of social and political immorality, which is a constant feature of the poem, and which is obviously intended to suggest a directly causal relationship between a corrupt admini-stration and Court and a degenerate people, reaches what is per-haps its satirical climax near the very end of the poem:

> Scarce can our fields, such crowds at Tyburn die,
> With hemp the gallows and the fleet supply.
> Propose your schemes, ye Senatorian band,
> Whose Ways and Means support the sinking land;
> Lest ropes be wanting in the tempting spring,
> To rig another convoy for the k—g.
>
> (242–7)

Whereas Juvenal had merely feared that all the iron needed for agriculture would be unproductively used as fetters for criminals, Johnson's allusion to 'rope' wittily juxtaposes an overcrowded gallows at Tyburn and George II's visits to Hanover on behalf of his very un-English interests and German mistress. Not only is the King, as MacDonald Emslie has said, 'deserting the floundering nation, just in time, by ship',[15] but 'sinking' in this passage also carries those associations of 'decline', 'decrease' and 'decay' which Johnson attributes to the word in his *Dictionary*.

The lines just quoted not only follow, significantly, the 'fiery fop', 'frolick drunkard', and 'midnight murd'rer' passages, but immediately precede the implied contrast with a more glorious past:

> A single jail, in Alfred's golden reign,
> Could half the nation's criminals contain.

And it is this glorious past, peopled by such monarchs as Alfred and Elizabeth, which the corrupt present shames and threatens to obliterate. When Thales views the nation overrun with foreigners, he exclaims:

> Ah! what avails it, that, from slav'ry far,
> I drew the breath of life in English air;
> Was early taught a Briton's right to prize,
> And lisp the tale of Henry's victories;
> If the gull'd conqueror receives the chain,
> And flattery subdues when arms are vain?
>
> (117–22)

In a previous passage the poetical friend, going even further back in time, invites 'Illustrious Edward'—Edward III, the victor at Crécy as Henry had been at Agincourt—to survey once again this former land of saints and heroes. The 'rustick grandeur', the 'surly grace', is no longer to be seen. Not merely enslaved but even emasculated by its traditional enemies, the nation presents a sorry contrast to its former greatness:

> Behold the warrior dwindled to a beau;
> Sense, freedom, piety refin'd away,
> Of France the mimick, and of Spain the prey.
>
> (104–6)

That Edward III has no historical counterpart in Juvenal's third satire is indicative of the fact that Johnson more obviously shows

a poet's sense of history in developing his theme. In the first ten
lines of the poem, for example, he significantly opposes to London
those strongholds of the ancient Briton—Wales, Scotland and
Ireland. To Thales the present corrupt capital is an alien city, and
he therefore resolves to fix his home 'on Cambria's solitary shore'.
His journey to Wales is prompted not by a desire for rural retirement so much as by a readiness to associate himself with the spirit
of his country's ancient inhabitants. A 'true Briton' (l. 8), he cannot brook living in the capital under an administration that adopts
a servile policy towards Britain's traditional rivals. Unwilling to
compete in lies and flattery with a 'fasting Monsieur' (l. 115) or
'supple Gaul' (l. 124), he is appropriately described as 'injur'd' (l.
2)—a word that Johnson's *Dictionary* invites us to gloss as not only
'wronged', but 'annoyed', 'affected with inconvenience'. Thales
has been wronged by the loss of that freedom which was his
birthright. And so, with a backward glance at the 'neighb'ring
town', he addresses the poet in words of burning indignation:

> Here let those reign, whom pensions can incite
> To vote a patriot black, a courtier white;
> Explain their country's dear-bought rights away,
> And plead for pirates in the face of day;
> With slavish tenets taint our poison'd youth,
> And lend a lye the confidence of truth.
>   Let such raise palaces, and manors buy,
> Collect a tax, or farm a lottery,
> With warbling eunuchs fill a licens'd stage,
> And lull to servitude a thoughtless age.

(51–60)

Here we notice an important difference between Thales and Juvenal's poetical friend. Admittedly Umbricius is also conscious of
the dignity of the simple, agricultural life of the ancient Roman
stock, as well as of the present degenerate state of life in the
capital. He finds it insulting to be forced at every turn to give
place to ingratiating foreigners; and because of his scruples he is
unable either to accept contracts for degrading occupations, or

to share the bosom secrets of despicable men in high places. Yet he is, in a sense, merely cutting his losses by proposing to retire to the country, for every day finds his stock of capital depleted in a city that offers no reward for his honest labours. Johnson's Thales, on the other hand, though he hints at the lack of personal return in the corrupt city, inveighs more sternly against its vices. His tone never takes on the occasional jaunty astringency of Juvenal's satire. He is

> Resolved at length, from vice and London far,
> To breathe in distant fields a purer air.

(5–6)

Moreover, Juvenal either treats the prospect of retirement ironically—as when he says (in lines not translated by Johnson) that 'it is something, in whatever spot, however remote, to have become the possessor of a single lizard'—or seems at least prepared to indulge this notion, as in the conclusion of his poem. There Umbricius expresses his willingness to leave his retreat whenever his friend should wish to read him satires at his own place in the country. These lines suggest little more than a literary companionship between like-minded friends living in country retirement. But Thales' 'numbers' are, on the contrary, self-confessedly 'angry' (cf. l. 259), and his final words may be said to ring with a more active spirit of opposition:

> Then shall thy friend, nor thou refuse his aid,
> Still foe to vice, forsake his Cambrian shade;
> In virtue's cause once more exert his rage,
> Thy satire point, and animate thy page.

Thales is, then, Johnson's portrait of a 'true Briton' in the contemporary sense of that term: his refusal to sell his birthright and succumb to political oppression shows that he still has the good of the nation at heart. It was in this sense that, two months after *London* was published, Pope used the word with a nice irony in his *One Thousand Seven Hundred and Thirty Eight*: *Dialogue II*:

Here, Last of *Britons*! let your Names be read;
Are none, none living? let me praise the Dead.

(250–1)

And several years earlier, in a letter to William Pulteney, a leading
opponent of Walpole, Swift had, with characteristic brevity, be-
queathed to his friend 'an epitaph for forty years hence, in two
words, *Ultimus Britannorum*' ('the last of the Britons').[16] It is therefore entirely appropriate that Johnson's description of the country
should carry overtones of that romantic past celebrated by earlier
chroniclers and poets. With Thales' resolve to become a 'hermit'
(l. 4) and 'Give to St. David one true Briton more' (l. 8), it is interesting to compare a passage from Drayton's *Polyolbion*, a poem of
which Johnson himself was 'extremely fond'.[17] In the Fifth Song,
Drayton describes as follows 'holy *Davids* seat':

Of all the holy men whose fame so fresh remaines,
To whom the *Britons* built so many sumptuous Fanes,
This Saint before the rest their Patron still they hold:
Whose birth, their ancient Bards to *Cambria* long foretold;
And seated heere a See, his Bishoprick of yore,
Upon the farthest point of this unfruitful shore;
Selected by himselfe, that farre from all resort
With contemplation seem'd most fitly to comport;
That, voyd of all delight, cold, barren, bleake, and dry,
No pleasure might allure, nor steale the wandring eye.

(333–42)

At St David's Thales would find the perfect hermit's retreat.[18]
There his 'safety', like that of the ancient Briton who 'in poverty
defy'd his foes' (l. 48), would be assured, whether his enemy were
the foreign invader or, as the poem more expressly implies, those
forces of corruption which, so rife in Court and city, constitute,
in themselves, a form of invasion.

Indeed, Thales' sense of oppression is so acute that he would
even be willing to contemplate emigration—supposing, that is, he
might be able to find some 'secret island' or 'peaceful desart yet

unclaim'd by Spain' (ll. 172–3). But England's foreign policy of
course makes this impossible. He therefore proposes that his companion should, like himself, find a refuge in some corner of their
own neglected country:

> Could'st thou resign the park and play content,
> For the fair banks of Severn or of Trent;
> There might'st thou find some elegant retreat,
> Some hireling senator's deserted seat;
> And stretch thy prospects o'er the smiling land,
> For less than rent the dungeons of the Strand.
>
> (210–15)

In this passage, which is one of the more striking examples of the
beatus ille theme in English literature, Johnson depicts the modern
Briton's equivalent of Horace's Sabine farm. Its mood has much
in common with Horace in his more stoical moments, for the
poet is celebrating neither pastoral ease for its own sake nor un-
committed retirement. The country not only offers a refuge from
vice but imposes a duty. Since the whole land is in need of reju-
venation, the hireling senator must be replaced by such men as
are prepared to provide anew the backbone and moral fibre of the
nation. Thales therefore goes on to suggest the contribution that
the eighteenth-century patriot can make by substituting a virtuous simplicity for corrupting luxury, sturdy independence for
sycophantic dependence, and restored vitality and beauty for
moral ugliness and decay:

> There prune thy walks, support thy drooping flow'rs,
> Direct thy rivulets, and twine thy bow'rs;
> And, while thy grounds a cheap repast afford,
> Despise the dainties of a venal lord:
> There ev'ry bush with nature's musick rings,
> There ev'ry breeze bears health upon its wings;
> On all thy hours security shall smile,
> And bless thine evening walk and morning toil.
>
> (216–23)

Certain references in this *beatus ille* passage have a more or less direct bearing on the political theme expressed by Johnson's country-city antithesis. The 'hireling senator' or 'venal lord' may be taken to represent one of Walpole's toadies who has sold his birthright for a seat in a government bent on ruining the nation. Moreover, since London, situated on the Thames, has been lost to liberty and virtue, the poet is forced to celebrate instead the second and third rivers of the kingdom. The Severn, especially, was an appropriate dwelling-place for the modern Briton to choose. According to a tradition utilized by both Milton in *Comus* and Drayton in his *Polyolbion*, Sabrina, the goddess of the Severn, was a descendant of the Trojan founder of Britain. The modern Briton who inhabited her banks would therefore have been acknowledging his descent from his spiritual forbears. The allusion to the Trent is, perhaps, more personal. Miss Lascelles has noted that Lichfield, Johnson's birthplace, was a country town 'built round a confluence of springs and streams feeding the Trent'.[19] What more understandable than that this young provincial, to whom Walpole's policies were obviously so repugnant, should have associated the natural seat of the true modern Briton with his own corner of England!

The satire on Orgilio, arguably the poem's only full-length portrait, has also been interpreted as an inept rendering of Johnson's source-material. In the words of the Yale editors of the poem,[20]

> . . . *London* suffers from an undeniably academic quality. The imitation of Juvenal assumes the nature of translation and conflicts, like the Orgilio of the poem, with the English satire. Johnson admitted this fault, but was probably too engrossed in other work to change it.

The only evidence for this statement is Johnson's later manuscript note, written on the 1750 quarto text of the poem, stating that this portrait 'was by Hitch a Bookseller justly remarked to be no picture of modern manners, though it might be true at Rome'.[21] As I shall try to show, the Orgilio portrait is an altogether subtle adaptation and effective reworking of the Juvenalian source in that it makes the distinctively political theme of Johnson's poem even more emphatic and pointed. The extent of this cannot, in fact, be fully appreciated unless it is recognized that this portrait was intended to represent none other than Walpole himself.

Orgilio is mentioned twice in *London*, and in each instance this name must refer to the same figure. Line 84 reads, 'Who shares Orgilio's crimes, his fortune shares,' where Orgilio is a substitution for Juvenal's Verres. In the second passage, beginning at line 194, Orgilio stands for Juvenal's Persicus or the master of 'the great house of Asturicus' (*magna Asturici . . . domus*). Both substitutions will be considered in turn and the appropriateness of their application to Walpole suggested.

During Walpole's administration, the most influential Opposition paper was the *Craftsman*. In its pages, as Dr J. H. Plumb has remarked, 'Walpole and his ministry were subjected to an endless stream of vilification and criticism which made not only England but Europe roar with delight'.[22] The dedication ('To the People of England') prefixed to the first volume of the collected edition of this work (1731-7) frankly acknowledged Walpole in his public capacity as Prime Minister to be its prime target. And to this first volume was also prefixed a motto from Cicero's famous indictment of Verres, the implication obviously being that what could be said of the wicked governor Verres could equally be said of Walpole as a second Verres. Nor was this all. In 1737 the eighth volume appeared, containing one paper (No. 259) which undertook to spell out in plain English, for the benefit of female readers, the meaning of the earlier motto from Cicero. Here Verres is clearly meant to stand for Walpole. He is represented as a man 'already condemn'd by the *general Voice of the People*', as 'a *Plunderer of the Treasury*', and 'an *Invader of the antient Rights of the City*' (p. 25). He is even said to have 'busied himself very diligently, as if he had been born and bred nearer to our Latitude and Times, in plundering and harassing the poor People, over whom he presided' (p. 24). No contemporary would have failed to see that a likeness to Walpole was here intended, even though the author prudently made the satire more oblique by comparing his ostensible subject with the *'whoreson round Man'* and knight, Sir John Falstaff. Sir John and Sir Robert, we are asked to conclude, were alike in both their physical dimensions and moral character, for Sir John was similarly deemed to be a *'Robber of the Ex-chequer'* who publicly invited 'his *Prince* to take share of the Plunder' in the same way that Verres himself 'always distributed a Share of the Booty among his *chief Officers* and *Projectors of his Jobs'* (p. 26). In Johnson's later words, 'Who shares Orgilio's crimes, his fortune shares.' This practice of reading Walpole for Verres thus makes it more than probable that Orgilio as a translation of Verres represented none other than the hated Walpole.

Clearly readers of poetry were practised in making such substitutions since Pope's *One Thousand Seven Hundred and Thirty Eight*, published within days of Johnson's *London*, also strongly hinted at the identification of Walpole with Verres. Lines 51–2 of the first edition read:

> *Agysthus, Verres*, hurt not honest FLEURY
> But well may put some Statesmen in a fury.

And in revised editions of his companion piece of the same year, Pope again invited readers to link Walpole and Verres:

> But let me add, Sir ROBERT's mighty dull . . .
> But pray, when others praise him, do I blame?
> Call *Verres, Wolsey*, any odious name?
>
> (133, 136–7)

The first edition had read 'Clodius' for 'Verres', but the revision is an improvement. For Publius Clodius, the unscrupulous and profligate tribune, Pope substituted that enemy of the people and national interest who could easily be identified, along with Wolsey and Walpole, as a type of the wicked statesman.

It may be here noted that it was also customary to regard Walpole as a type of Wolsey,[23] and that this fact is probably not without its relevance for Johnson's portrait of Orgilio. The name itself is suggestively symbolic: Johnson's *Dictionary* defines 'orgillous' as 'proud', 'haughty' (though it surprisingly does not record the more usual form 'orgulous'). And the accepted prototype of the proud or orgulous statesman was Wolsey. Johnson's *Vanity of Human Wishes* refers with some historical justification to his 'full blown dignity' and 'pride of aweful state' (ll. 99ff.) since parliament had, in preferring its very first article against Wolsey in 1529, objected to his 'high, orgullous, and insatiable mind'.[24] Might not Johnson have therefore expected his readers to interpret Orgilio as a satire on a second Wolsey as well as on a second Verres? A clear precedent for this had also been furnished by the *Craftsman*: paper No. 8 had compared Walpole and Wolsey in terms of their *superbia* or pride. The gist of its motto, from Seneca's *De Tranquillitate Animi*, is as follows:

> Those whom an unkind lot has placed in a critical position will be safer by reducing their pride in the things that are in themselves proud (*superbiam detrahendo rebus per se superbis*), and by lowering their fortune to the common level.

The details of Wolsey given in this paper are clearly reminiscent of Walpole also. Wolsey, though 'of a *low Education*', rapidly made a fortune of which his use was 'extravagant and ostentatious to the highest Degree': 'he built *Palaces*; and his Train out-shone his *Master*'s so much, that when he retir'd into the Country, on a Party of Pleasure, the Court became desart' (*Craftsman*, I. 46). Similarly Walpole, through his triumphant manipulation of power and finance, obliterated all vestiges of his provincial past. He built at lavish expense the magnificent Houghton Hall in his native Norfolk, to which 'his colleagues—dukes, earls, barons—rode post haste . . . at his call'.[25] His levees, held three times a week, were thronged with noble supplicants, and by 1733 he controlled under his own hands all diplomacy, finance and patronage. Ambassadors and consuls also, apparently, knew their duty, and gratified with expensive gifts Walpole's passion for paintings and sculpture.[26]

Johnson's extended portrait of Orgilio represents his translation of that passage in Juvenal's satire which describes the destruction by fire of the *magna Asturici . . . domus*. If, as I believe, Walpole's Houghton provided the inspiration for the English equivalent of this Juvenalian passage, then the destruction of Orgilio's 'palace' is necessarily represented as hypothetical since no 'just bolts' from heaven destroyed Walpole's palatial residence. Yet the imagining of such an event as a parallel to the Latin original at least allows the poet appropriately to suggest the 'sudden wealth' that produced Orgilio's 'golden pile'. The political overtones of this passage are, in fact, obvious.

> The laureat tribe in servile verse relate,
> How virtue wars with persecuting fate.
>
> (198–9)

This couplet does not appear in Johnson's manuscript, which instead contains the lines:[27]

> With servile grief dependent nobles sigh
> And swell with tears the prostituted eye.

Such nobles could not have been 'dependent' on anyone except Walpole, and prudence doubtless dictated that this couplet should not appear in the published version. Again, Orgilio's 'gaudy vassals'

> The price of boroughs and of souls restore,
> And raise his treasures higher than before.
>
> (204–5)

And another couplet clearly refers to Walpole's placemen:

> With well-feign'd gratitude the pension'd band
> Refund the plunder of the beggar'd land.
>
> (200–1)

On such a reading the 'beggar'd land' represents England itself, of which the wealth would naturally have seemed to the political satirist to flow straight into Walpole's own pockets.

Arguably Johnson never intended this portrait to be read without any political overtones as a simple substitution for Juvenal's Persicus. Nevertheless, it seems certain that he wanted his readers to remember the Latin example, for his letter to Edward Cave prior to the poem's publication insisted that the corresponding passages from Juvenal should 'be subjoined at the bottom of the Page, part of the beauty of the performance (if any beauty be allow'd it) consisting in adapting Juvenals Sentiments to modern facts and Persons'.[28] Through the example of Persicus, Juvenal was attacking that social evil of imperial Rome whereby rich and heirless old men and women were shamelessly courted by fortune-hunters (*captatores*) who hoped for a large legacy in return for their persistent favours and attendance. Thus this 'most sumptuous of childless men' (*orborum lautissimus*), when his house is destroyed by fire, has it rebuilt with even greater splendour from the costly gifts contributed by legacy-hunters.[29] This social evil, as Hitch remarked, had no exact counterpart in contemporary London: though Johnson's *Rambler* contains various portraits of the captator-like tactics of distant relatives hot on the scent of a fortune, Juvenal's scorn was, in a broader sense, directed at that childless society of imperial Rome which, by disregarding marriage, fostered such an insidious form of dependence. It was this kind of difference that presented a problem for the Augustan 'translator'; as Johnson was to observe in his later *Life of Pope*: 'Between Roman images and English manners there will be an irreconcilable dissimilitude, and the work will be generally uncouth and party-coloured; neither original nor translated, neither ancient nor modern'.[30] As a young poet, however, he had himself brilliantly solved the difficulty that the example of Persicus presented by extending Juvenal's implied satire on dependence, and accommodating it to his own distinctive theme. Orgilio-Walpole, by fostering a kind of dependence even more dangerously insidious, was perverting in favour of a host of sycophants those honours which should rightly have been the prerogative of merit and the birthright of every true Briton.

Apart from a possible reference to George II and another to either 'Orator' Henley, a propagandist hired by Walpole, or to Lord Hervey, Queen Caroline's confidant and Walpole's most trusted agent in the palace, Orgilio is the first figure satirized in the poem. And apart from the contemptuous reference to the King in line 247,[31] he is also the last. Such an arrangement, especially when taken together with the poem's other political allusions, has the effect of tending to concentrate the satire towards a single point. In associating a general moral turpitude with political corruption, Johnson was not, of course, breaking unfamiliar ground: Pope's version of Donne's fourth satire presents in vivid and unmistakable terms the effect of the courtier's gossip on the unwilling poet:

> Nor more Amazement seiz'd on *Circe*'s Guests,
> To see themselves fall endlong into Beasts,
> Than mine, to find a Subject staid and wise,
> Already half turn'd Traytor by surprize.
> I felt th' Infection slide from him to me.
>
> (166–70)

But in view of the necessary obliquity of Johnson's attack, it is interesting to note the terms in which Swift had expressed in a letter to Pulteney his sense of the corruption of public morals:[32]

> It is altogether impossible for any nation to preserve its liberty long under a tenth part of the present luxury, infidelity, and a million of corruptions. . . . Such hath ever been human nature, that a single man, without any superior advantages either of body or mind, but usually the direct contrary, is able to attack twenty millions, and drag them voluntary at his chariot-wheels.

A clearer statement of the same sentiment had appeared in *Craftsman* 413:

> If a *Minister* should be exalted here, with a Disposition to mind nothing but the Increase of his private Fortune, and

consequently aim at nothing so much as to continue Himself in his Employment, tho' the Means were ever so flagitious . . . our Ruin would follow as certainly from Him, as it could from any other. If He singly set about this Work, by playing our own Corruption upon us, by reducing all the Corporations into a venal Habit, by bestowing only upon such as were qualified to elect Members of Parliament the inferior Employments, and afterwards by confining the larger and more lucrative to the Parliament, thus chosen, and to such of its Members, as would accept them upon the base Tenure of doing all his Drudgery; if This should ever happen, the Increase of our Corruption must easily be foreseen. (XII. 230)

The author of this paper goes on to envisage the loss, not only of morals, but of liberty itself, in a passage that could well have stood as a motto for Johnson's poem.

The above reading of *London* enables us to view in a new light its structure and theme. The Yale editors seem wrong to suggest that its 'topical elements' are not as essential 'structurally' as those of the *Vanity of Human Wishes*;[33] while the 'plan' of the poem is clearly not 'jejune', as one critic has claimed.[34] In *London*, the corruption of the whole city is imaginatively linked with the current political scene: its 'vice' is ultimately of political origin in that 'the dregs of each corrupted state' become 'the cheated nation's happy fav'rites' (ll. 91ff.). Moreover, the juxtaposition of ideas in lines like 'Ere masquerades debauch'd, excise oppress'd,' or 'Behold the warrior dwindled to a beau,' reflects a significant feature of the poem's total organization. The praise of 'illustrious Edward' and Britain's former 'rustick grandeur' follows immediately on Johnson's contemptuous reference to 'a French metropolis'; and this contrapuntal arrangement of material is especially evident in the second half of the poem, where the *beatus ille* passage both follows on the portrait of Orgilio, and precedes the 'fiery fop' and 'midnight murd'rer' paragraphs. Here the mutually exclusive alternatives facing the still virtuous citizen are significantly juxtaposed.

Thales, seeking to preserve intact his moral character and his liberty, emphatically dissociates himself from the corrupt city and exhorts the poet to do likewise. The country, as the antithesis of all that Orgilio-Walpole stands for, has become the logical home of this 'true' though 'harassed' Briton. And, given the use to which this antithesis is put, it is surely probable that the sympathetic contemporary reader—like Walpole's opponent George Lyttelton, who carried a copy of the newly-published poem in high glee to Pope—would have been fully aware of the political significance of its various allusions. Indeed, he might well have been impressed by the anonymous poet's originality in rewriting his Latin model to give such a devastatingly trenchant picture of the contemporary scene.

Notes

1 *London: A Poem and The Vanity of Human Wishes, with an Introductory Essay* (London, 1930), esp. pp. 15–17.
2 *Samuel Johnson* (New York, 1944), p. 64.
3 *Samuel Johnson* (London, 1954), p. 8.
4 *Boswell's Life of Johnson*, ed. G. B. Hill, rev. L. F. Powell (Oxford, 1934–50), I. 129.
5 *English Satire and Satirists* (London, 1925), p. 230.
6 *Op. cit.*, p. 63.
7 'Johnson and the Classics', *New Rambler*, June 1965, p. 15.
8 'Johnson and Juvenal', *New Light on Dr Johnson*, ed. F. W. Hilles (New Haven, 1959), p. 41.
9 *Boswell's Life*, I. 129.
10 *The Poems of Samuel Johnson*, ed. D. Nichol Smith and E. L. McAdam (Oxford, 1941), p. 2.
11 *The Politics of Samuel Johnson* (New Haven, 1960), p. 90.
12 See *The Works of Samuel Johnson, LL.D.* (Oxford, 1825), VI. 91, 103–4; X. 166; *The Political Writings of Dr Johnson: A Selection*, ed. J. P. Hardy (London, 1968), pp. 13–14. For a revealing comparison

of Johnson's version of Carteret's speech during the Lords debate with that recorded by Archbishop Secker, as well as with that which appeared in the *London Magazine*, see B. B. Hoover, *Samuel Johnson's Parliamentary Reporting* (Berkeley and Los Angeles, 1953), p. 64.

13 D. J. Greene, '"Logical Structure" in Eighteenth-Century Poetry', *PQ*, XXXI (1952), 332.

14 *Of Dramatic Poesy and Other Critical Essays*, ed. Watson, II. 145–6.

15 'Johnson's Satires and "The Proper Wit of Poetry"', *Cambridge Journal*, VII (1953–4), 351.

16 *The Correspondence of Jonathan Swift*, ed. Harold Williams (Oxford, 1963–5), IV. 303.

17 W. B. C. Watkins, *Johnson and English Poetry before 1660* (Princeton, 1936), p. 7.

18 The suggestion that Thales should be identified with Richard Savage, who left London for Swansea in July 1739, fourteen months after *London* was published, takes no account of the sense in which Thales is described as a 'hermit'. F. V. Bernard, reopening this question, has suggested resemblances between Savage and Thales: 'Savage was single, profligate . . . line 4 refers to him (i.e. Thales] as a "hermit"; line 20 mentions his "dissipated wealth"' (*NQ*, CCIII, 1958, 398). Johnson's *Dictionary*, however, defines a 'hermit' as someone who is 'single' in a very special sense: '1. A Solitary; an anchoret; one who retires from society to contemplation and devotion. 2. A beadsman; one bound to pray for another'. The further suggestion that Thales' 'dissipated wealth' refers to Savage's profligacy does violence to the context in which these words occur. Thales' wealth has been 'dissipated' by 'malice, rapine, accident'.

19 'Johnson and Juvenal', in *New Light on Dr Johnson*, p. 44.

20 *Samuel Johnson: Poems*, ed. E. L. McAdam, Jr, with George Milne (New Haven and London, 1964: The Yale Edition of the Works of Samuel Johnson, vol. VI), p. xviii.

21 *The Poems of Samuel Johnson*, p. 5.

22 *Sir Robert Walpole: The King's Minister* (London, 1960), p. 141.

23 For extensive documentation of this see C. B. Ricks, 'Wolsey in *The Vanity of Human Wishes*', *MLN*, LXXIII (1958), 563–8.

24 See Edward Herbert (of Cherbury), *The Life and Reigne of King Henry the Eighth* (London, 1649), p. 266.

25 Plumb, *Sir Robert Walpole*, p. 249.

26 Cf. *ibid.*, pp. 85–6, 98, 266.

27 *Samuel Johnson: Poems*, p. 57. It is interesting to note that Johnson's MS. had read 'Sejano' for 'Orgilio' at line 208—a reading that makes the suggested identification with Walpole even more plausible.

28 *The Letters of Samuel Johnson*, ed. R. W. Chapman (Oxford, 1952), No. 7.
29 Juvenal is here, of course, indulging in rhetorical exaggeration: as we learn from his other satires, such parasites usually bought their obsequious gifts in the meat-market! Juvenal's is, however, an exaggeration that makes the Walpole parallel appear even more convincing.
30 *Lives of the Poets*, ed. Hill, III. 247.
31 See *ante*, p. 107.
32 *Correspondence of Swift*, IV. 303.
33 *Samuel Johnson: Poems*, p. xviii.
34 Greene, ' "Logical Structure" in Eighteenth-Century Poetry', p. 331.

Index